"In my domestic and overseas travel, I've met families who serve both God and country far beyond what most civilian families can imagine, often at great personal and family sacrifice. Ellie Kay has written a practical, biblically based, down-to-earth book filled with inspiration, ideas, and practical suggestions for military families. I'm thrilled to see this encouraging book available to this worthy audience."

—Dr. Jay Kesler, Chancellor, Taylor University

"With wit, wisdom, and compassion, Ellie Kay has given us a book that inspires the highest form of patriotism. *Heroes at Home* is filled with stories that will capture your heart, but the author moves the reader beyond inspiration to understanding how to provide 'hands-on' help to American military families. The practical applications woven with poignant illustrations will make this book a classic manual for every American who wants to 'do something' to help our country."

—Carol Kent, President, Speak Up Speaker Services, international author and speaker

"Serving in the military presents husbands and wives with unique challenges when it comes to marriage and family. Husbands and wives need a strategy to make sure their relationship doesn't become a casualty. Ellie Kay is a veteran who has learned how to adjust to the challenges of making a marriage work in this environment. This book can point you to a plan that works for military families."

—Bob Lepine, Co-host, *FamilyLife Today*

"*Heroes at Home* is a book that begged to be written, waiting for none other than Ellie Kay to write it! You'll not find a more helpful, supportive, patriotic, passionate, and empathetic woman working alongside her man in uniform (with five kids underfoot) than Ellie. At least not one who can save you money on one page, make you laugh out loud on the next, and by the end of the book inspire you to stand up proudly, a tear in your eye, to salute our military men and their families who make incredible sacrifices to defend our liberty. God bless America; God bless the hands that penned this book; and God bless the unsung heroes who read it."

—Becky Freeman, National speaker, bestselling author

"Commanders at all levels know how essential it is for the 'rear echelon' to have a 'state of readiness' not unlike the deployed forces. Ellie Kay has captured this essential need in *Heroes at Home*. It is a wonderful tool for service spouses, but also should be read by service members. The greater understanding of the challenges that the rear echelon faces in separation, moves, and the unusual demands of departure, reentry, and family management, the better those heroes will be ready to support the forward deployed. Yes, spouses of America's Armed Forces are truly the *Heroes at Home*."

—Brig. Gen. Dick Abel, USAF (Ret), Executive Director, Military Ministry, Campus Crusade

HEROES
at HOME

HELP & HOPE
for AMERICA'S MILITARY FAMILIES

ELLIE KAY

BETHANYHOUSE
www.bethanyhouse.com

Published by Bethany House Publishers
11400 Hampshire Avenue South
Bloomington, Minnesota 55438

Bethany House Publishers is a division of
Baker Publishing Group, Grand Rapids, Michigan.

Printed in the United States of America

Library of Congress Cataloging-in-Publication Data
Kay, Ellie
    Heroes at home: help and hope for America's military families / by Ellie Kay.
      p.   cm.
    ISBN 0-7642-2789-0 (pbk.)
    1. Families of military personnel—United States. I. Title.
UB403 .K38 2002
355.1'2'0973—dc21
                                                2002015282

To Lenn Furrow
Your encouragement empowers
Your example inspires
Your kindness continues.

ELLIE KAY is a bestselling, award-winning author, national radio commentator, and regular media guest as well as a gifted speaker. She is a graduate of Colorado Christian University with a degree in the management of human resources. She and her husband, Bob, a contract fighter pilot with a major aerospace corporation, have five children at home and two adult children and make their home in Southern California.

If you wish to contact Ellie Kay for speaking engagements, media, or seminars, she can be reached at:

Ellie Kay
% Speak Up Speaker Services
1614 Edison Shores Place
Port Huron, MI 48060

speakupinc@aol.com
E-mail: *ellie@elliekay.com*
Web site: *www.elliekay.com*

~ BOOKS BY ELLIE KAY ~

The Debt Diet
Heroes at Home
Money Doesn't Grow on Trees
The New Bride Guide
Shop, Save, and Share
A Woman's Guide to Family Finances

~ACKNOWLEDGMENTS

There's always a story behind a book, and *Heroes at Home* is no exception. It's been a book idea I've had for some time. There just wasn't anything out there that provided specific help to a military family's unique needs. I have tried for years to get this book into print, but it wasn't time—until now. It started as a spur-of-the-moment article that I submitted to Tom Neven at *Focus on the Family Magazine.* The article was read by millions of families, and I was encouraged that perhaps *now* would be the time for this book to happen. I want to thank my literary agent, Lee Hough, for assisting me in pursuing this idea and for his direction in the process.

Bethany House Publishers had the vision to bring help and hope to thousands of military families around the world through this book. I want to thank them for helping to educate America about what it means to live this lifestyle. I consider them family.

My key contact at Bethany House for this project has been Steve Laube, Editorial Director/Adult Nonfiction, whom I've known since the beginning of my life as a published author. Not only did Steve acquire and present the manuscript but he also edited it under a tight deadline and was a constant cheerleader when the pressure threatened to overwhelm me. You've made the effort to know me and my work, and for that I thank you very much.

Rachel St. John-Gilbert is the freelance editor who provided another set of eyes on this project and helped me in the tough spots. She's got a great sense of humor, and whenever I write "we" instead of "I," she reminds me with a question: "Who is 'we'? You and Sybil?" In addition to being a super editor, wife, and mother, Rachel is also quite the fisherman. I thank you for your wit and wisdom.

Saving the best for last, I want to thank my precious family for putting up with a crazed woman on a short deadline. My "Beloved" is also my hero, Bob Kay. Thank you for being the "World's Greatest Fighter Pilot" and for allowing me the freedom to bloom where I've been planted. I thank our children, Daniel, Philip, Bethany, Jonathan, Joshua, Missy, and Mandy for your prayers, flowers, coffee, colored drawings, and notes saying, "I love you, Mama!"

And to the hidden heroes, the military family members at home. Thank you for the sacrifices you make to support the people who defend our nation's freedoms. I salute you.

THIS BOOK IS FOR ALL AMERICAN PATRIOTS—MILITARY or civilian. The military family will read this and learn how to do things a little better or smarter, while civilians will learn what it's like to live the unique and often challenging lifestyle of an American military family. My hope is that it will help *all* of us learn how to be better patriots by not only supporting those who serve our country but also by learning how to better understand and support their families.

Over 4.2 million Americans are serving or have served in our nation's military defense, and those numbers are on the rise as the war on terrorism continues. There are a number of heroes among that number, and the most highly decorated individuals will invariably attribute their heroics to a team effort: the humble assertion that there are other people who stand behind the strength, courage, and daring of these individuals. These men and women deserve their medals, but behind every hero is a unit, a team, or a family—their support consists of people both on and off the battlefield. Without this support, they couldn't be as focused and on top of their game as they need to be. For example, pilots can be taken off flying status if there is intense turmoil at home, and a soldier could have trouble concentrating on her mission if her family is hurting.

Of the 4.2 million military members, nearly 60 percent are married with families, and it is to that select group of Americans that this book is dedicated. Their stories are hidden, oftentimes unknown to anyone outside their four walls. Some of these spouses have married into the military not fully knowing what they're getting into. I have found that military family members tend to quickly develop four characteristics in order to survive above and beyond the call of duty: (1) a keen sense of humor; (2) a sense of adventure; (3) the ability to develop courage in a variety of challenges; and (4) a strong sense of family.

Humor is at the top of the list: a graduating senior tipped his cap to reveal a taped-on message: *Semper Fi* (the Marine motto meaning "Always Faithful"). They have to look at life in a lighthearted way in order to cope with the heavy stress that accompanies this incredible lifestyle. Many learn to laugh *at* themselves and *with* others, and in the process they find a way to rise above the circumstances that surround them.

Military families are also *adventuresome*. They may have to pack up their entire fold-away home into eight huge crates and move it to another country, where they don't know the language or the culture—and then do it again in six months.

Courage also describes the military family. The new bride of three months who sends her twenty-year-old husband into an unknown venture, while she lives out the separation far from family, learns to be pretty gutsy by the time she celebrates her first anniversary. Faith often undergirds the courage needed to tenderly kiss your spouse good-bye, not knowing when you will see him again or *if* you will see him.

Because they are likely far from extended family, the military's appreciation for immediate *family* is naturally heightened. Often siblings are the built-in playmates that provide continuity amid numerous moves. Absence from the military member also tends to make the heart grow fonder (not to mention the cool gifts Mom or Dad bring back from other countries). The real challenge is to learn to say, "Hi, Mom (or Dad)! I'm glad you're back home!" before yelling, "What did you bring me?"

Humor, adventure, courage, and family—these could very well describe the hero in a blockbuster summer action film! In many ways these families are heroes. They don't get the Navy Cross or the Bronze Star, but they deserve a medal—it could be called the "Hidden Heroes" award: They're heroes at home.

When military members know that their spouse can hold things together at home, and when they have confidence that their spouse believes in what they do for a living, they are better able to concentrate on their duties. Sometimes that concentration is the difference between life and death.

When Americans support those who support our troops, they play a key role in our nation's defense. This book is designed to educate Americans about military families, because while these families are unique, they are common in their need for affirmation, encouragement, and helping hands. This is also a guidebook for ways that military families can do things more efficiently and effectively.

Every family member is impacted when Mom or Dad takes the pledge to defend our country and risk his or her life to do so. A three-month-old baby sacrifices when that parent is called away, elementary-aged children pay a price for freedom as they adjust to talking to Mommy or Daddy over a video hook-up. Teenagers, at a time when they need their parents most, also miss a deployed parent (although many would rather eat strained spinach than admit it). Finally, the spouse left at home sacrifices by putting on the single-parent hat along with the many other hats they already wear. This book is a tribute to everyone who has loved someone in the service and supported that one in whatever way they could. *You* are the hero. You may be hidden, but it doesn't diminish the effects of your contribution. America salutes you!

Celebrating
Hidden Heroes

CHAPTER ONE

Hidden Heroes

The Top Ten Qualities of a Hidden Hero

D*uring the final days of the Gulf War, I took our three-year-old son, Daniel, his two-year-old brother, Philip, and our infant daughter, Bethany, to watch their father launch his F-4 Phantom II. He was going to the Middle East. His mission: to fight for our nation's freedom.*

"When will de Papa be back home, Mama?" asked Daniel as he waved his chubby hand at the roaring jet.

"Soon," I said as I fought back tears and kissed my baby daughter on her fuzzy blond head. "We are praying he will come home soon."

Philip was excited; he loved watching airplanes: "I wuv you, Papa!" he shouted as he jumped up and down. Then all of a sudden he turned to me, furrowed his brow, and said very seriously, "You know, I weally wuv de Papa." Then he turned to wave at the small speck in the sky as his dad flew off to his mission.

Later that week Mrs. Phillips, Daniel's Sunday school teacher, told me that Daniel had a special prayer request. She said he asked, "Please pway for all de air farce guys dat fly to betect our fweedoms." Then he paused and added, "And please pway for dem Army guys dat do de same thing—but dey fly and fwight on dem helicopters. Oh, and pray for de Army gulls, too!"

★   ★   ★

Daniel didn't quite understand what his father did for a living a decade ago, but after the Kosovo war and now with our current situation— he does. As a military family who currently has five school-aged children and two adult children, we have a keen appreciation for what it takes to keep this nation free. We've lived through these two wars and know that my husband, Lt. Col. Bob Kay, will likely be called upon again to fly and fight in order to protect our nation's freedoms. The kids and I are the veterans on the home front.

Some have called military families the "hidden heroes at home," but most of us would not accept such a distinction. After all, we don't wear the uniform, we haven't sworn to offer our life's blood to defend our nation, and we don't eat MRE rations in some faraway place. We merely support those who do.

And yet if Bob knows that when he returns from his mission he will have a loving family waiting for him, he is better equipped to perform at the height of his capabilities. When he believes that his family will have people in the community who will assist them through the uncertain weeks and months ahead, he rests a little better when he contemplates the stars in a darkened sky half a world away. And in many ways, these families, as well as their communities, have contributed to our national defense, as have all the supportive families of other airmen, sailors, and soldiers.

★   ★   ★

I have always disliked the distinction "the little woman," who stays at home, wringing her hands, waiting for her husband to come back. Military spouses tend to be proactive, courageous, and every now and then a little goofy (in a patriotic kind of way). There are plenty of things we can do ahead of time to prepare effectively for those long and short separations. While we can't be sure the kids won't get sick or the washer won't break down, we can do some preventative maintenance in order to help things run smoothly while our heart anxiously awaits the return of our loved one.

There are some basic things military families can do to be more prepared for the various aspects this lifestyle presents. While some of the things listed here seem pretty basic, others, such as relationship issues, are not as evident. And yet these other aspects of our lives have a great impact on how we are able to cope with the moves, the separations, and the financial constraints. Later in the book there will be dozens of specific helps for the areas we're discussing in this chapter. But for now here's a general overview of your adventure as a military family.

Network of Military Support

Plug into your unit's individual family readiness group; if not actively, then at least in a casual way. You don't have to head a fund-raiser committee or be the driving force in this group, but attend a few coffees or activities. You will need this group when your spouse deploys—for information disbursement as well as support.

Network of Non-Military Support

When families live on base/post, their children attend the base school, and they go to the base chapel. They can easily become "base cadets." We need to broaden our scope of influence and our children's through developing relationships with non-military friends. We need a break from military-speak, and these friends can provide that bit of touch with reality. Consider joining groups off base/post or go to a civilian church to make sure you have friends who will keep you balanced.

Legal Limitations

If your spouse is going to deploy (it could be for a month that turns into a year), you will need to check with your installation's legal department and get your wills in order and a power of attorney. Make sure that your name is on your checking and savings accounts and that your name is also on the title to your vehicles and your home. These simple precautions can save you major financial and legal problems.

Budget Binges

If you don't have a budget, look at one of the chapters in section 5 of this book to see how you can get one set up for your family, and then get on a budget right away! Be sure you know about the finances in your home and that you have the power of attorney to handle all the financial decisions that could arise when your spouse is deployed. You might also want to budget for "Fun Funds" to be used when your spouse deploys. This would cover those binges such as extra eating out, going to the movies or a theme park, or even buying a new outfit. If these are funded, they won't be a liability to your budget.

Learn It, Don't Burn It!

I've heard of more than one person who burned up a car engine because they didn't change the oil! During sustained deployments, your local Family Support Center equivalent often has programs to help you maintain your vehicle. In the meantime, learn the basics of car maintenance (or where and when to take it to have this service done) and home maintenance. You are quite capable of simple home repairs if you decide you're going to learn how to do it. The key is to learn to be flexible.

For example, when we were stationed in northern New York, I took a snowblower class in early September. Later in the month Bob went TDY to Florida, and we had our first snowstorm—but I was prepared. I simply took our handy-dandy John Deere snowblower and cleared our driveway. Then my neighbor Joy asked me to clear hers—so I did. By the time I was finished with her driveway, Elke, my neighbor across the street, was yelling over the wind, asking me to do her driveway. By the time I finally shook the snow off my boots and went inside in time to get the kids ready for school, my husband's operations officer called and asked in an "I'll help the little woman out" way: "Would you like me to come over and snowblow your driveway?"

I squared my shoulders, smiled sweetly, and held the phone firmly in my hand as I replied, "No, thanks, I've already cleared our driveway—and two more!"

It's pretty cool to be equipped to blow your own snow (or do other routine maintenance chores). But you have to prepare *before* the storms come.

Scheduled Play

Have a plan for some rest and relaxation before your spouse deploys. Interview baby-sitters, find a reliable friend you can swap kids with, look over the course schedules offered by the local community college or civic center, join a choir or an aerobics class. But it's critically important to have scheduled play times for YOU while your spouse is away. If it's not immoral or illegal, build it into your schedule. This will keep you from frantically scrambling at the last minute, when you're at your wit's end, looking for someone to watch the kids or trying to find a break that is yours alone to enjoy.

Mend Fences

If you or your spouse has "unfinished business" with each other or with extended family members, peace time is THE time to get these issues worked out. It may be hard and may even require the assistance of a counselor or base/post chaplain, but it is vitally important that you make every effort to mend these fences. If you've at least tried, you can have a clear conscience that you have done your part. Encourage your spouse to do the same with his/her extended family members.

Don't Burn Bridges

Remember the classic saying "What goes around comes around"? Well, it's true! Bob found himself to be outranked by guys that he once hazed as a sophomore at the Air Force Academy. Boy, did HE ever regret acting like a jerk back then! Conversely, one of the cadets that used to work for Bob, and who kind of had a few run-ins with him over parking tickets, found himself face-to-face with his old Air Officer Commander when the young pilot graduated from pilot training and went to fighter lead-in school. As a matter of fact, this pilot was in centrifuge training, out of state, when his young wife went into labor three weeks early! They had no one else to call to coach her in childbirth, so they asked me to go to the hospital. The pilot made it back just after his son's birth, and was he surprised to see who helped deliver the baby!

The truth is no matter what walk of life you're in, you never know when the tables might be turned, and a past acquaintance is in a position to either help you or hurt you. So it's a good idea when you run into "difficult" people to just walk away—don't get even. You might end up living near them at some point, or worse, your son might marry their daughter!

Top Ten Qualities
of a Hidden Hero
★ ★ ★

1. **Sense of humor** An ability to laugh at oneself and with each other.

2. **Flexibility** What it's called when you create an elaborate candlelight dinner and farm out the kids for the night, and your husband calls to say he's not coming home because they have an inspection coming up.

3. **Courageous** The ability to wave good-bye for the two-hundredth time, fight back the tears, smile, and say, "You come home safely; I'm proud of you!"

4. **Extraordinary** An ability to move fifteen thousand pounds of household goods in twenty-four hours.

5. **Strong** Nerves of steel (for all those close calls and near misses).

6. **Patriotic** Unashamed to shed a tear during the presentation of the colors or the singing of the national anthem.

7. **Faith-Full** Brimming over with faith in God and true to your country.

8. **Independent** Confident during solo parenting gigs, but ready to move to interdependence when the spouse comes back home.

9. **Acronym Reader** The ability to decode three-letter acronyms (TDY, PCS, UOD, MRE, OIC, SOF, BDU, SOL, etc.).

10. **Superhero** The capability to conquer new lands, stay in touch with old friends, keep the home fires burning, jump buildings in a single bound, and stay out of the funny farm.

CHAPTER TWO

Angels Among Us

Practical Ways to Help Military Families

~

Got your backpacks?" *I shouted above the clamor of five children in the car as they prepared to go to school.*

Yes!

"Lunches?"

Yes!

"Homework?"

Yes! and Um . . .

"Um? Did I hear an 'um'?" As "Drill Sergeant Mom," I glared at my seventh-grade boy and said calmly, "Go get it!"

He scrambled out of the car, while the others fought over who got to talk to Dad first when he called later that night from his deployment to Red Flag. And I quietly wondered how "roughing it" in Las Vegas constituted "serving your country." But as my homework cadet reported in from parole, it was time to continue the roll call.

"Permission slips?"

Yes!

"Water bottles?"

Yes!

"Shoes?"

Yes! and Um . . .

"Um? Did I hear an 'um'?" Once again the drill sergeant cast her steely eyes on the guilty party. This time I zeroed in on my youngest, our first-grade son (aka "Turbo Dude" for his ability to hustle, which of course comes in handy when he's so forgetful!).

"You forgot your shoes again?!" I exclaimed as he squirmed under my

laser-beam stare. *"And if I hadn't asked you about it, you'd end up at the drop-off zone at school like you did last week—Shoeless Joe Jackson! Now go get them, quickly!"*

The little guy scrambled out of the car, grabbed his shoes off the shoe rack in the garage, and "turboed" back into the vehicle at record speed. I fondly observed my "baby" and mentally counted the days until his dad would return home to play checkers with the chubby-cheeked cherub. This was day one, and there would be twenty-nine more days of this particular absence.

With the roll call complete, this temporarily single mom began to back the huge white Suburban out of the garage, when suddenly she heard a sickening scrape of metal on metal, followed by her children's screams:

Mom, STOP!

"Oh, no! No!"

You hit the garage door! It fell off the tracks and landed on the back of the car!

"Oh, no! No!"

I lost it along with the kids. "Who left the garage door partially open?" I asked incredulously. The automatic door lifts it all the way up, and some-one had to have purposefully stopped it before it was raised!

Suddenly the whole car became oddly quiet, and then one little voice broke the silence. It was the voice of Sweet Pea, our eight-year-old nearly perfect child.

"Um . . . Mama? Papa said that when the weather is hot like this, we need to leave the garage door partly open. Since Papa is gone, I'm doing his job, and I left it partly open." A wave of tears filled his huge hazel eyes and spilled down his cheeks. "Did I do something wrong?"

Letting out a huge sigh and mustering a semblance of control and the kindest reply I could manage, I answered, "Well, Sweet Pea, I know you're being a big helper. But your dad meant the garage should be partially opened from the bottom when we're at home, not partially opened from the top when we're leaving."

Only twenty-nine days to go!

★   ★   ★

As a veteran wife and mom, I've seen my share of "accidents" at home while Dad was away. Any military spouse will tell you that it seems as soon as the troops deploy, the children get sick, the washer breaks down, or a distracted mom absentmindedly plows through a partially opened garage door. We've purchased *two* garage doors in the past year. Overhead Custom Doors now carries our door in stock, ready for the next deployment!

But how do you describe what a deployment is to those who don't know? MCpl Ed Thompson is a husband, father of three, and a serving member of the Canadian forces. Here's his definition:

> Most often we think of deployments as a time when a member departs for an extended period to some far-off exotic land. In fact, a deployment includes any time a member is separated from their family, such as a two-week assignment in sunny Wainwright or a yearlong assignment to the Middle East. So when you think of deployment, don't just think of our men and women serving overseas, but also think of those who are away from their families on course, training exercise, and assignments.

I have the confidence that the Kay family will survive these continued separations, even though it doesn't feel like it at times. We have in the past, and we will in the future. One of the ways we manage is through the help of "angels with skin on." These people put their faith into action and come to the rescue when daily routines become unbearable and the mundane issues of life—like mowing lawns and cooking dinner—threaten to be my downfall. They are the angels that walk among us, and their help is simply heavenly.

We all have our limits. Doing the single-mom thing while worrying about my spouse's safety will at times create so much tension that the thought of plowing through the week without help is almost too much to bear. It is precisely at these moments that God provides a strong back to take care of a few of Dad's chores, or we receive a hot meal when I'm too exhausted to cook.

In times of national concern, people ask themselves (or the military family) how they can reach out in practical ways to help the heroes at home. Americans really do care about each other, as is most evidenced during times of national tragedy. Often people—even extended family members—don't know how to help; that's what this section is for. It will help you help others to help you.

The other problem military families have is that sometimes well-meaning people think what they're doing is helping when it really isn't. For example, the in-laws that want to come and welcome the ship back into port. That seems like a very natural thing to do, and to suggest otherwise could be deemed ungrateful. However, a closer look at the nature of military separations and reentry issues indicates that it would probably be better if the in-laws gave the sailor a couple of weeks to readjust to his nuclear family before they come to visit. That's why a copy of this book in the hands of your family and friends will help you and a lot of other military members.

Here are some suggestions that you may want to pass along to those who want to be angels with skin on from those who think the *right kind* of help is simply divine!

Phone Calls

Initially there are quite a few phone calls, cards, and letters of support when military members deploy or when the TDY begins. This can be a great source of encouragement, but here are a few tips to make the most of your support:

Brevity. Keep the initial phone calls brief and to the point, such as: "I just wanted to let you know that we're here for you and want to support you in any way we can."

Sensitivity. Be mindful that sometimes people will want to talk and other times they won't, because they can feel bombarded by phone calls as well as the enormity of their circumstances.

Leave a Message. Due to the number of phone calls, some families may have an answering machine on at all times. If you get the machine, don't hang up; just leave a short message expressing your care and concern.

Visits

If you are related to a military family, your initial reaction might be to go and help them. Here are some items to keep in mind if you are considering a visit. These guidelines can also be photocopied and mailed to your extended family members so they will know how to best help you.

Ask First. Don't call your daughter or nephew and simply announce your intentions to come to their rescue. Ask permission to come and be prepared for a "no" or a "please, not right now" answer.

It's Not About You. If you get one of the two negative responses about a visit, remember that this is not all about you. Don't make life harder for these family members by insisting on your so-called "family rights" or "responsibility" to help.

Asset, Not Liability. If the military family feels that your visit would be a real asset during this time, carefully consider the living arrangements. If your family lives in military housing, it is more than likely very small. Consider staying at an inexpensive hotel, at billeting on base/post, or even renting an RV to stay in during your visit. Close quarters can make for added stress.

Permissive Help. If it is determined that you will go to visit your family, then decide to help without taking over. I've had many friends whose families show up and then let the mom do all the cooking for the additional family members! Ask permission to help; then once you get a green light, by all means clean, cook, do laundry, take the children to the zoo, mow the lawn, change the oil in the car, fix the broken door handles, run errands . . . well, you get the idea.

Keep Those Cards and Letters Coming

During Desert Shield, our troops sat in the desert for six months for a three-day ground war. Once the media frenzy of the initial deployment wears off, people get on with their lives and tend to forget the families that remain alone for many weeks. Here are ways not to forget:

Mark Your Calendars. Make a weekly reminder note to send a card or make a call. A small note makes a *big* difference.

Humor Helps. Humor can be an incredibly healing balm and provide a much-needed release, so you might want to send a funny card, a poem, cartoon, book, photo, or family-oriented video.

Unconditional Love. Do not require a response from your friend. Your card may have meant a lot, but your friend may be so distracted by the stress of the deployment that they may forget to thank you (at least right away). The usual protocols do not always apply during sustained separations from family members.

When in Doubt, Send Chocolate (or Other Tokens of Support)

Okay, this piece of advice comes from a chocoholic, but the logic is sound—give the heroes at home small gifts from time to time. These special treats can make all the difference during a difficult stretch. Small acts of kindness reap big rewards to those holding down the fort at home.

Money Is No Object. Thoughtful reminders that someone is thinking of you don't have to be expensive. Drop off a gift basket filled with your friend's favorite foods (did I mention chocolate?) or a video rental of a movie they've been wanting to see (be sure to let them know when it's due back).

Gifts of Time. I've been called the "Coupon Queen" many times, but why not make a coupon booklet as a gift? Include coupons for free baby-sitting, a meal, a favorite batch of cookies, a coffee date, running errands—the possibilities are only limited by your imagination!

Group Gifts. Groups of friends (such as a Sunday school class or work group) could join together and buy a long-distance phone card, a gift certificate for a favorite restaurant, or movie passes for a fun night out.

Saving Private Ryan

It can mean a lot to the family at home to know that others are keeping in touch with the military member. Here are some practical ways to reach out:

Prayer. There's an old saying "There are no atheists in foxholes." No matter what the military member's religious affiliation is, the overwhelming majority of people won't turn down prayer. Let them know you're praying for them regularly.

Prayer/Letter Chains. If you want to take the above tip a step further, organize a group of friends to pray each week. Have the weekly prayer partner write a note to the military member to let him/her know they're praying. But be sure it's all right with the service person before you organize this chain.

Letters. Your family can adopt a single service member. Send photos of your family, drawings from your kids, and letters of appreciation for the service they are rendering our nation.

Gifts. Check with the military member and see what restrictions there are on small gifts. One suggestion is a book called *Taking the High Ground—Military Moments With God* by Col. Jeff O'Leary (Cook, 2001). This book is bringing comfort and wisdom to thousands of veterans, military members, and their families. It gently gives them hope and points them onward and *upward*.

Angels With Skin On

It's one thing to give a family an open-ended statement: "If there's anything we can do to help, please let us know." Chances are they will never call for your help. Here are some ways to be proactive in your offer for help:

Refusals Permitted. While you offer help, be sensitive to the fact that they may refuse it. Don't take it personally; just make another offer to help at a later time.

Be Specific. Instead of a blanket proposal for help, offer a tangible form of assistance, such as "May my son and I come and mow your lawn on Friday or Saturday?" Or, "I'd like to bring you a meal one day next week. What day would be good for you to take a break from cooking?"

Group Projects. If your group wants to help, have specific projects in mind. For example, a youth group could clear away all the leaves in the yard. Remember, always have adult supervision and be responsible for those in your group. These projects can be a tremendous blessing to the families involved.

Chapter Three

Hidden Hero Portrait—
Myra Hinote

She's Cool, She's Clever—And She's Got a Really Clean Car

~

*T*he base was conducting an exercise, alternating the security require-ments between FPCON (Force Protection Condition) Bravo and the more serious FPCON Charlie. Just as any able-minded person wouldn't dare make jokes about guns and bombs while walking through metal detectors at an airport, you wouldn't make jokes when going through the base security check at the main gate. But Myra wasn't really able-minded: her husband had deployed for the eighth time in six months and she was fending off three very cute (but very active) preschoolers. In a court of law, I'm sure any jury would declare her temporarily insane after seven straight nights of nursing sick kids with colds and ear infections.

Myra drove up to the security gate in a squeaky clean van—she'd just been through the car wash for the third time in three days. It seems that Hunter, her three-year-old son, found life's fulfillment by going through the small town's brand-new, automatic, triple deluxe wash system—with colored bubbles! (Who says those marketing researchers didn't know how many minivans they could clean with that sly tactic?) Every time they'd drive by the facility (which happened to be several times a day because it was on the main drag in town), he'd announce from his car seat:

"Car deedy, Mama!"

Just in case Mama hadn't heard how dirty he thought the car was, he'd shout it again.

"Car deedy, Mama!"

Myra ignored him and drove her daughter to school.

"Car deedy, Mama!"

She went by the drive-in cleaners and pulled out her credit card.

"Car deedy, Mama!"

She pulled into the drive-thru bank. He yelled into the teller's microphone, "Car deedy, Mama!"

Moms are good at ignoring kids—for a remarkably long time. But any mom who is honest will tell you that it begins to wear on you about the thirty-second time.

"Car deedy, Mama!" Hunter was no quitter. But Myra was—especially when she was doing the single-mom thang.

Much to Hunter's delight, his life was once again fulfilled for the day as he giggled and shouted over the colorful bubbles. Their van was squeaky clean as Myra drove by the security forces guard at the gate during Threatcon Charlie.

The young airman sported an M-16 on his back as he approached Myra's open window. He wore his Battle Dress Uniform (BDU), which was especially hot on this sweltering day in the New Mexico desert.

He was in no joking mood.

Myra was so relieved that she had a temporary respite from Hunter's endless chattering. She absentmindedly pulled her identification out of her wallet for the guard, who now stood in front of her window.

"Ma'am, we are in Threatcon Charlie; may I see your military identification?"

Myra smiled smugly at her efficiency (who says mothers of young children don't have it together?). She had the card ready; the guard wouldn't have to tap his foot impatiently while she searched for it in her purse.

She thrust it through the window so the policeman could see it clearly.

He looked shocked at first, eyeing Myra suspiciously. Then he took one look at sleeping baby Holly and glanced over at Hunter in his car seat (who was, once again, shouting you-know-what).

For the first time that day, the guard smiled.

"Well, ma'am, that's a really nice credit card, but I'll need to see some other ID."

★ ★ ★

Myra is *not* your typical security gate criminal offender. She was offered a scholarship to Berkeley, accepted to MIT, and graduated from Wellesley with a double major in astrophysics and religion. This background came in really handy when she married her husband, Clint, the number one graduate in his class at the U.S. Air Force Academy. They ended up living in the middle of a sandy desert in New Mexico with three babies under five. While her classmates are getting partnerships and advanced degrees, she's establishing support groups and chairing fund-raisers for nonprofit organizations.

Does this sound like the life she always envisioned?

No.

Are her days full of joyful (and not so joyful) surprises?

Definitely.

Is she happy?

Are we grading on a curve? Okay, well, most of the time.

Myra is cool, courageous, and clever—she's even got a clean car. She's a hidden hero.

"If I felt that life stopped when the guys deploy, I'd have no life!" That's her basic philosophy regarding TDYs, school, and deployments.

When they were first married, Clint was assigned to Columbus, Mississippi, a small town of around thirty thousand people. For some strange reason there weren't a lot of job openings for astrophysicists who could give running commentary on the world's major religions. So she did what tons of military spouses did: she adapted. When life gave her lemons, she made lemonade—out of chocolate, no less! She turned her hobby of "truffling" into a full-fledged business and became a successful chocolatier, marketing her "to die for" truffles in dark chocolate, raspberry, kahlua, and orange flavors.

In order to verify the truthfulness of this, I asked Myra (okay, so I demanded, begged, and groveled) to:

"Just hand over the chocolate, and no one gets hurt."

So she did.

Now, I have to tell you that I am a chocolate connoisseur; I've tasted so many "Death by Chocolate" creations that I should have passed on long ago (but what a way to go!). I've sampled Godiva, savored Parisian chocolates, and drooled over the best chocos the Belgian Alps had to offer. But NOTHING is as good as Myra's! (I might have to sample a few more just to make sure.)

The week she "charged" through the base gate, she also spearheaded a fund-raiser for a support group called *MOPS* (Mothers of Preschoolers), a group she took to the next level in their second year. As the coordinator and head of the steering committee (or "the leader of all leaders," as one five-year-old put it) of this nonprofit organization, she doubled the membership, thus meeting the needs of dozens of moms with young children throughout the community. Her background as a gourmet chocolatier came in handy as well. She even organized the creation of 2,000 truffles for the fund-raiser!

Fiercely independent, Myra put her computer skills to work by free-lancing for an entrepreneurial Web site designer, who handles some of the best association and industrial sites on the Internet. It's one way she maintains her personal identity despite being a traveling mom who has moved five times in seven years.

Myra is now facing every hidden hero's fear: sending her husband to fly F-16s in Korea for a year by himself. She is going through the roller coaster emotions that are intensified by the fact that the Air Force may not send him after all. There usually seems to be a Plan B, C, and D. But it's Plan E—the one that no one ever thought of—that comes through most often.

Myra is trying to decide whether she's going to leave the network of friends she's established at her present base and move for that year to be near family. She would be leaving the kids' preschool, her home, friends, church, network of activities, and volunteer work in order to be near family. She would have to establish a new home, find a new school, make new friends, and search for a new church. It's hard for civilians to understand this aspect of military life and the incredible challenge that accompanies it.

One Family Services director employs an excellent exercise to help educators understand what their military students experience on a regular basis. You might try this exercise to help family members, co-workers, or other civilians gain an understanding of the lifestyle. If you're reading this and you are non-military, just follow the directions.

Step One Think about all the things you enjoy most in life right now. These must be things that are on the outside of your home, and they cannot be your own family. For example, you may enjoy the way your neighbor laughs over coffee, the southwest sunset you see from your balcony, or the great gym that you work out in.

Step Two Narrow your list to the top three.

Step Three If you are in a group setting, have the exercise leader collect all the slips of paper from the participants.

Step Four The leader tells the audience, in a soft, soothing voice, "Thank you for listing these and for passing them forward." Most of the audience expects her to read them aloud, thinking they might guess who wrote them. But instead, the leader does something very unexpected with the slips of paper.

Step Five The leader takes all the responses, walks over to the side of the room, and throws them in the trash can as she announces: "You've just moved to a new place and *no one cares.*"

★ ★ ★

Sure Myra's family cares, but the strangers she meets in the new neighborhood, school, grocery store, church, and gym don't know her. They don't care. They don't understand why she's married but doesn't have a husband within six thousand miles. She's starting all over *again.* What magnifies the difficulty of all the military spouses in Myra's situation is one major factor: *She must do all of this alone.*

There will be

- no one to take turns getting up with the baby (and that baby may not recognize Dad when he comes home next);
- no one to fix the garbage disposal;
- no one to go out on a romantic date with (what romantic dates? I settle for just going out!);
- no one to accompany her to the principal's office;
- no one who can meet her at the doctor's clinic;
- no one to share the funny little thing that Holly did or Hunter said— only the other parent can find some of these things to be indescribably endearing;
- no one for Hunter to play catch with;
- no one sitting at the other end of the dining room table;
- no one to take Meg to the father/daughter banquet;
- no one to share her laughter;
- no one to kiss her tenderly;
- no one to wipe her tears;
- no one who even *knows* she cried herself to sleep;
- no one to snuggle at night.

For an entire year—she is alone.

★ ★ ★

Myra is coming to terms with this monumental event that lies in her not-too-distant future. And just about the time she compartmentalizes, internalizes, and strategizes a way to deal with it—good old Uncle Sam may change the game plan. That's why "flexibility" is a necessary characteristic of life as a hidden hero.

But where is Myra today? I had a chance to ask her just that.

Ellie: Are you worried about your future?

Myra: Long term, no. Short term, I sure have my doubts!

Ellie: Have you decided what you're going to do?

Myra: Yes, finally, after months of agonizing. I'm planning on moving to North Carolina and going back into the chocolate business.

Ellie: How do you think you'll handle this separation?

Myra: I'll take it one day at a time—with God's grace and a decision of my will to never give up and never give in.

Ellie: Myra, you may design the next award-winning Web site while building lifelong values into your babies that will help them change the future! Or you *may* eventually teach astrophysics on the university level. I've got a feeling you'll go wherever your feet and faith take you. Do you have any regrets about being a military family?

Myra: Maybe a few twitches of longing here and there, especially when I read my alumni magazine from college. Because my classmates are getting advanced degrees, becoming partners in law firms, and achieving a lot out there. Then one of my kids laughs or runs up to give me a hug, and I think, "Not on your life."

Ellie: Are there some days when you would trade your entire life for a good book and five minutes of solitude?

Myra: You bet my deedy car I would!

★　★　★

At the end of your life you'll never regret not having passed one more test or not closing one more deal. You will regret times not spent with a child, a husband, a friend, or a parent.

—First Lady Barbara Bush

In an address to the 1990 graduating class of Myra's school, Wellesley College

Celebrating Family

CHAPTER FOUR

Bunny Tales
Creating Memories and Managing Holidays

*E*ver since she was old enough to hold a crayon and find an empty wall, our daughter Bethany has been in the creative business of writing and drawing. She earned the nickname "bunny" because when she was two years old, she made us read ABC Bunny and No, No, Bunny from the Cottontail series about a total of a gazillion times.

She not only enjoyed reading, she adored creating too. By the time she was five years old, she had comprised some five thousand, two hundred and forty-seven works of art. We posted them on our refrigerator, my desk, Bob's work computer, and even the toilet seat cover. I couldn't bear to throw them away, so I shipped them by the boxful to grandparents and aunts and uncles as our way of keeping in touch with family. But just like another bunny we know, she kept going, and going, and going. . . . Bethany's creations multiplied as quickly as bunnies do, and I knew if she ever found any of her treasures in the trash it would traumatize her.

What's a mother to do? Well, I started including them in the payment envelope when we mailed the bills—the gas, electric, and phone company all received brightly colored pages from her "Peter Cottontail" coloring book, carefully signed, "Love, Bunny."

I was committed to valuing her self-esteem, so I brought along a few with me in the van when I ran errands. The teller at the bank got a picture of a bunny hopping through the tulips. The dry cleaners proudly displayed "Flowers and Puppies" on their window. Even the auto mechanic took down his Sports Illustrated cover to put up her "Mama Kitty" drawing and didn't even charge me for repairing our flat tire!

When I got pulled over for speeding one time, I encouraged her to hand *one over to the police officer. She was only three at the time and sat proudly in her car seat, her blond hair gathered on top of her head like Pebbles from* The Flintstones. *She flashed her bright blue eyes and happy teeth as she thrust a coloring of a pink blob through the window.*

"What do you think that is?" she asked, convinced that the policeman had stopped us in order to get one of these treasures.

"Uh . . ." He was completely taken off guard as he looked into her bright, eager eyes.

"Uh," he repeated. "It looks like a pink . . . uh, thing?"

"That's right!" she squealed, "It's my pink shoe. I ride it. Like my brudders ride der bike! We can go now, Mama. The policey-man got his picture!"

I glanced over Bunny's head to the previously stern officer. My eyes saw a reflection of what he found in my daughter's—eager and bright.

He caved. Big time. The pressure of a Mama Rabbit and her Bunny was just too much. So instead of a much-deserved ticket, he gave me a warning.

"Ma'am. You were going 45 in a 30. You will need to slow down in the future. And, uh," he turned toward Bethany, "thanks for letting me catch up with you so I could get my picture!"

Unfortunately, that brush with the law only encouraged me. I began to stick her "cottage industry products" on the rearview mirror in the car, the bathroom mirror, and my compact powder mirror. So whenever I looked into a mirror, I saw a reflection of my little Bunny.

★　★　★

Bethany's outgoing personality suited our military lifestyle. Bob and I were geographically separated from family the second year of our marriage, and we've never lived within a thousand miles of our extended family since. So the new "friends" Bethany picked up along the way were there to encourage her (okay, they fawned over her) the way her grandparents would if they lived nearby.

Staying in touch with extended family members is just as important to the military family as it is to any American family, but it's often a challenge because of the distance. Sometimes military families just give in, charge three thousand dollars on the credit card, and run home to Mama. Others try to convince themselves that they "don't really miss having grandparents" and try to pretend they're all right, when they're really feeling lonely and disconnected from those they love. Still others give up trying to keep a relationship going with extended family and miss the joy of connection.

But it's not a hopeless cause. It takes an extra measure of work to keep that relationship with friends and family going when you live far apart. These relationships are important for us, for our kids, and for our future grandkids. Our children will see the way we've treated our parents, and they may one day treat us the same way! So investing in the lives of your extended family is investing in your future life with your children and grandchildren.

Another issue that arises for military families is the "holiday crisis," where they are torn between two (or more) sets of grandparents. This made one family say, "We're just not going to see anyone this year, or next year, because it will make one set of parents mad; so we're not doing anything at all!" These are difficult choices, but there are some proactive ways to decide whom to spend time with and still stay within your budget. You can set the boundaries for your nuclear family and explain these to the extended family.

Here are some ways to strengthen the roles of extended family members in your lives, stay connected between visits, and tips on handling the holidays.

Building Memories. Take some of those works of art that your children have created and build a "Creative Memories" type portfolio for your extended family. Attach photos to the artwork. If your children are old enough, have them write the captions, a short story explaining what they're doing in the picture, or even a poem that expresses their feelings about their family. You can send these to relatives monthly or hold the keepsakes until the end of the year and present them at Christmas as a special memory book. Don't forget school papers, certificates, or special awards that you can photocopy and include.

Family Calendars. Your local discount department store's photo department is a great resource for making this a truly personal gift. Take photos year-round and order a gallery calendar for your extended family. Write as many special days as you can on their calendar, including birthdays, first and last days of school, moving day, promotions, beginning of the various sports seasons, or even anniversaries. This reminds extended family that their military family is thinking of them, and it might even encourage them to make phone calls, send notes, and be more involved in the lives of those they love from afar.

Kids' Mugs. If you're related to a military family, consider having your photo printed on a mug. Kids love to have their own special cup, and each time they drink from it, they are reminded that they have family who thinks they are special. This even helps very young children recognize and stay connected to Grandma and Grandpa.

Holidays

Where to spend the holidays can be a great challenge for hidden heroes. It can be costly to travel to see family, and yet there's always the possibility that instead of living one thousand miles away, you'll be ten thousand miles away next Christmas. Consequently, a sense of "now or never" can impact these decisions and can also be a cause for dissension among the ranks.

Let's take a look at the case study of a sailor we'll call Tom and his wife, Sally. The "holiday decision" was one of the most volatile topics in Tom and Sally's first year in the military. But a lot of the tension could have been eliminated if this couple had taken the time to sit down and discuss the holidays long before the season arrived.

Let's face it, the old saying "You can please some of the people some of the time, but you can't please all of the people all of the time" is never more true than when it comes to where you are going to spend the holidays. When you add stepparents, siblings, and grandparents, you can become torn in so many directions that the joy of the holiday can be drained away. The goal is to come up with a plan that is acceptable to both spouses so that everyone comes out a winner.

An exercise that will help get the conversation started toward a win/win result is to get out a sheet of paper and write down each holiday that could possibly be spent outside your family nest.

Next, list the way you would like to spend each holiday individually. This column will likely be largely based on what your family traditions were like while you were growing up. Also list the feelings you have associated with the holiday. Finally, you will have to compromise with lots of understanding and be willing to use positive communication techniques to decide what you will do for each holiday as a couple.

Some of the questions Tom and Sally had to consider were: (1) Do you want to simplify the season? (2) go to parties and be with people? (3) stay within a limited travel budget? (4) spend the day in the comfort of your own home?

Take a look at the following sample of Tom and Sally's list. It is easy to see why it led to a doozie of an argument.

This couple is an extreme case because their expectations for the holidays and diverse backgrounds were on opposite ends of the spectrum. But if they reached resolution, so can you. By sitting down together and discussing the holiday topic, you can avoid future arguments on the same topic and put to rest any smoldering ashes left over from the last disagreement. As you can see from the final column in our chart, each side had to give and take in order to reach a consensus.

In their discussion, they took into account that the decisions they made in the "here and now" would affect their future children and the rest of their family. So they made their decisions based on what would maintain peace, create lasting and loving memories for their own family, and be an asset to their relationship. They also kept in mind the fact that any decision would not be set in stone but could be modified to meet their future real and felt needs, geographical location, and family situation.

Maybe the plan will get you started on how to celebrate your holidays this coming year and for many happy years to come.

Holiday Celebrations Work Sheet/Year of _____

Thanksgiving Day

Sally	Tom	Compromise
1. Watch Macy's parade	1. Sleep in late	1. Tom sleeps; Sally gets her cocoa and watches the parade
2. Lots of food, fine china, and dressy attire	2. Camp out at home in grubbies	2. Every other year they will have a traditional dinner at the relatives' house. The alternate year is spent at home with a turkey menu
3. Traditional menu	3. Pizza or whatever	
4. Spend entire day with extended family	4. Watch football games all afternoon	
5. Each family member shares two things they are thankful for	5. Get to bed early after eating the leftover pizza	3. They share what they are thankful for
		4. Alternate Christmas/Thanksgiving with relatives (when within traveling distance)

Christmas

Sally	Tom	Compromise
1. Christmas Eve church services	1. Open presents on Christmas Eve	1. Go to services, when available, and open one gift on Christmas Eve
2. Up at 6:00 A.M. to read Christmas story from the Bible	2. Sleep in late and wear pajamas most of the day	2. Tom sleeps in, and they read the Bible story when he wakes up (by 10:00 A.M.)
3. Open presents one at a time, thanking between each one	3. Few presents (the holidays were downplayed)	3. Three gifts, opened one at a time
4. Formal dinner at Grandma's house	4. Pizza or whatever (maybe tacos)	4. They realize the holiday can have the significance you give it
5. Ice-skating in the afternoon	5. Watch football games and then take a nap	5. Football in the afternoon and caroling at night (when possible)
6. Christmas-caroling at night	6. No particular traditions (Christmas is just commercialism)	

Thanksgiving

Thankful Tree

Our "Thankful Tree" was featured in a *Woman's Day* magazine one year. It took two photographers *eight* rolls of film and *four* hours to get *one* three-by-five photo in the magazine. Our youngest son, Joshua, who was then three years old, was missing for one roll of film, and we didn't notice until we saw him making faces from *behind* the photographers.

The tip we shared in the magazine is how we stay in touch with family and friends during this holiday. On November 1, we make a Thankful Tree on poster board and put it on our wall or front door. The tree is bare, because the leaves that we make out of construction paper have not yet been gathered. The leaves have the names of friends or individual family members on them and a place for the person to write what they are thankful for. For example, "Grandma Rawleigh is thankful for _____." But we leave the tree up bare at the beginning of the season to teach the children how barren our lives are without the giving of thanks.

We make and send the leaves to friends and family around the world along with a self-addressed envelope. When these envelopes begin to come back, the children get excited as they take turns opening them. At dinner that night, we read the leaf and give thanks along with those who are thankful and put the leaf on our tree. By Thanksgiving Day, we have a tree full of thanks. We carefully save the leaves in an envelope marked by the year and keep all of them in our Thanksgiving decoration box. Each year we read the leaves from past years.

We never know when this year's leaf might be someone's last, or which family might have a new leaf on next year's tree. So we give thanks.

Five Kernels of Corn

In the first year after our pilgrim forefathers came to America, there were periods of time when food was so scarce that the daily ration consisted of only five kernels of corn. In remembrance of these difficult circumstances upon which our nation was founded, each of our family members receives five pieces of unpopped popcorn and takes turns passing around a basket. As we drop each kernel into the basket, we name five things that we are thankful for this year. One friend who follows this tradition says that at the end of their thanks, "We pop the popcorn and rejoice in how God has 'multiplied' our blessings!"

Christmas

Photo Greeting Cards

We have photos made in October and get the savings of an early-bird discount on photo greeting cards. If you try this beginning in your first year of marriage, it will be fun to see how your family changes as the years go by. We even put together a special Christmas photo album, and it's a wonderful place to display our annual photo greeting cards and an effective way to preserve memories.

Simplify

The reason we keep our gift-giving simple is *not* because we're cheap. It's because we want to keep the focus on the Reason for the Season. Holiday mania detracts from the coming of the Christ Child as God's greatest gift to us.

Three Gifts

Part of the Kay Family Simplification Plan involves the number of gifts each of our children receive. This could also apply to each spouse, before the kids start coming along. I'll never forget one Christmas before we had children. Bob and I watched a little boy get so many gifts for Christmas that he got tired of opening them and quit. Sadly, he was so spoiled by his parents and grandparents that he had the mistaken notion that Christmas was all about him.

Sharing Christmas

Sometimes the gift of time is the greatest gift of all during the holidays. There are a number of ways you and your spouse can brighten the holidays of those around you and share the season. We like to visit nursing homes and spend time with the residents, talking and sharing. If you know of an elderly relative, neighbor, or friend who rarely gets to decorate for the holidays, why not help that person put up a tree and holiday lights? Then, after the season is over, help them put the decorations away.

One of the traditions on military bases is a holiday cookie drive. Last year we collected ten thousand dozen cookies and distributed them to the police department, the fire department, and others who worked the holiday shift. You could take a basket of goodies to your local firefighters or police officers on duty. I know they would enjoy these treats on Christmas Eve! We even bake cookies for the mail carriers and sanitation workers. We place these in easy-to-carry plastic bags and include a can of soda pop.

Mission of Joy

One final idea is to adopt a developing-country child at this time of the year and sponsor him/her year-round. A portion of the proceeds of my books goes to an organization that helps orphans in India called Mission of Joy. We also send out their brochures with every product order we receive on our Web site.

Jeff and Cindy O'Leary, the founders of this mission, have sacrificed the "extras" that many of their peers say are essential. They've seen God provide abundantly for their needs and for the orphans in India. The entire staff at Mission of Joy is made up of volunteers. They keep their monthly expenses at a minimum so they can send the maximum to where the needs are greatest—India. During its existence, MOJ has sent 97 percent of all contributions directly to India. Ask any nonprofit organization—that's an amazing percentage.

Mission of Joy will provide an Indian child with food, clothing, and education for a donation of $26 per month. You can contact Mission of Joy at P.O. Box 64914, Tacoma, WA 98464 or e-mail them at *jeffreyoleary@msn.com*. If you want to learn more about the history and current needs at MOJ, visit them on their Web site at *www.missionjoy.org*.

★ ★ ★

A gift is a demonstration of love from one heart to another. Calvin Miller once sent me an acrostic poem that spelled out my name. You cherish those special, personal gifts.
—CHUCK SWINDOLL
Tale of the Tardy Ox Cart

CHAPTER FIVE

Pilots Never Panic

Tips to Surviving Military Moves

⁓

7:00 On the morning of September 7, I woke up to get the children ready to take to the sitter because I had an appointment. I was having a few Braxton-Hicks pains.

7:30 My friend Pauline called from Colorado, and I asked her to pray that these contractions would get stronger and turn into the real thing on their own.

7:33 I hung up the phone, and the first hard contraction hit, followed by another strong one *three* minutes later. I remember thinking, *Wow! When Pauline prays, things happen!*

7:36 Daniel helped his younger siblings get into the van, and I drove them to the sitter's house and then headed a few blocks farther to the squadron.

7:40 At the squadron, Bob was about to fly, and he happened to be looking out the window when I drove into the parking lot.

He met my van outside. "Hi, Beloved (his term of endearment for me). Are you dropping off some bread for the guys?"

I put the van in park. "Yeah, honey, I'm dropping something—but it ain't bread!"

I was in between contractions. "This is it; I'm in labor!" I announced.

Even though he's had many children, Bob still panics every time I have a baby.

He stood there in his flight suit just staring at me.

I repeated, "Come on, let's go NOW!"

7:45 Bob ran back into the squadron, dropped his parachute, and shouted to the operations officer, "I'm having a baby!" Then he ran out.

7:59 Our van screamed into the hospital parking lot as Bob pulled into a "no parking" slot in front of the ER doors. With the engine running, he dashed into the emergency room, grabbed a wheelchair, and threw me into it.

8:01 Once inside, he ran the halls, ramming me into an occasional wall while turning a corner. I couldn't talk because there were only a few seconds between contractions.

Just then, to my relief, I saw the double doors at the end of the hall to Labor and Delivery. Rapidly my relief turned to concern, because the wheelchair wasn't losing speed, it was gaining momentum as Bob accomplished his mission.

My mind shouted, The door! It's an automatic door with a button on the side of the wall! It's not designed to be opened by the feet of women in wheelchairs!

Bob slammed the chair through the double doors, where we faced some shocked nurses. I heard him mumble, "Some automatic doors!"

"Wait a minute! Who are you?" they asked the zealous pilot and his human battering ram.

"I'm Bob, and she"—he pointed to me—"is going to have that baby right now!"

Then, like a drowning man coming up one more time for air, he bellowed, "Oh, my goodness! The van is still running and it's parked in the ER zone!"

In a flash . . . he was gone.

With the Red Baron out of the way, the nurses helped me to the bathroom to change. No sooner had I gotten the robe on than the baby slammed down the birth canal, and the nurses helped me to a bed.

8:02 One of the nurses shouted, "She's complete! Emergency delivery! Labor room two! Get Dr. Holzhauer—STAT!"

The other nurse asked, "Where's her husband?"

I answered in my mind, He's parking the car!

Thankfully, the doctor was in the hospital and arrived in seconds, out of breath from running. He knelt by my side and whispered, "All right, Ellie, I'm here."

8:05 With one intense effort, Joshua Steven was born.

8:10 Bob raced back into the room, shouting, "How is she?"

"Mister," said the southern nurse with a deep drawl, *"you done had yourself a fine baby boy!"*

He looked at his 10-pound 8-ounce *"Baby Huey."* Joshua earned the nickname *"Conan the Baby Barbarian"* because he always does things in a big way.

★ ★ ★

I wasn't the first military wife to give birth to a baby alone, and I won't be the last. Our situation was better than some, because at least Bob got there right after the birth. A friend of mine gave birth to their second child while her husband was flying helicopters in Viet Nam, and her military friends became her "husband." They coached, comforted, and celebrated with her the birth of that beautiful baby girl.

I wasn't fortunate enough to have my mom geographically nearby for any of our children's births. Just like my friend, I had substitute family in my military family, and for their support, they meant the world to Bob, our children, and me. They celebrated the births of our babies and provided meals and childcare for the other children, and I even found a couple of labor coaches among the crowd.

But this kind of "family" is never more important than when you're moving—especially if you're moving with a new baby. I remember when Bob worked at the Air Force Academy and we'd just had our fourth child, Jonathan, who was two weeks old. Bob came home *very* excited one day.

"Guess what, Beloved?" He didn't wait for my reply. "I get to stop flying a desk and go back to flying real fighters again! I've been asked to help stand up the AT-38 Squadron in Columbus, Mississippi." He paused only slightly for a quick breath and then delivered the punch line: "Can you move in two weeks?"

★ ★ ★

When you leave one military family, you're sure to find another in your new assignment. You know there will be others there who have pulled up roots more times than they can count. No sooner will you receive your farewell gift from where you are than you'll be sure to find someone on the other end waiting with a welcome gift. That's the beauty of the military family and their network of thousands of others around the world.

In fact, one of the greatest bonds military families have among themselves is the idea that we are from "everywhere and nowhere." While a precious few military families "homestead" or stay put in one area for anywhere from five to ten years, the overwhelming majority of us move more or as much as a traveling circus.

In order to gather a variety of perspectives as well as practical advice on the topic of staying connected while moving, I've compiled tips from all the branches of the service. There's so much good advice in this chapter that I'm actually looking forward to our next move! (Did I just *say* that?)

Here is a list of helpful ideas to consider for your next move, contributed by other heroes at [mobile] home:

Family Means "Home"

Home is where the herd is—the Kay herd, that is! Whether we're in a place three months or three years, it's important to make that apartment, set of quarters, or civilian house look and feel like home. Don't ever get into the misconception that you can live somewhere for a short amount of time without the touches of home. If you know you'll only be in an apartment for three months, make a point of keeping out at least a couple of boxes of your favorite photos, art, or other household goods to make it feel like home to you and your children. Yes, you'll have to repack them in just a few weeks, but during those weeks you will be surrounded by a few of your favorite things—and it will feel like home.

Code Two Move

A Code Two move is when your furniture is entirely bubble-wrapped and crated. Shrink-wrapping your couch is usually reserved for overseas moves. However, if *at the time you schedule the move* with the moving office you request a bid for a Code Two, it allows the local moving companies to bid on the move. If you wait until *after you've already scheduled the move,* it will be too late to process the request. If one of the movers will grant a Code Two move at a Code One price, you will have the advantage of greater care in the pack-up of your household goods.

Self-Moves

Before you decide to move yourself with a DITY (do it yourself move) and make a little extra cash—count the cost! We made one move when we were first married, hauling about five thousand pounds of household goods about one hundred miles to our new location, and we made over one thousand dollars (that was many years ago). That was certainly worth it for us! However, the next move was eight thousand pounds and one thousand miles, and after all the expenses of a moving truck, gas, and insurance, we would have only gained about three hundred dollars. The additional stress on our family and the sheer physical energy it would have taken for that move would *not* have been worth it!

Agencies

It is an absolute travesty to have the wonderful (not to mention free) resources we have in our military agencies and not use them! Work closely with your military point of contact for the move. If you are going overseas, you need to be sure to read all the information and checklists regarding visas, passports, and allowable household goods. It will vary from country to country. If you are moving CONUS (Continental United States), or even if you're moving overseas, go to your local Family Support Center/Army Community Services equivalent and request a SITES brochure, which will give you all the information you need to know about your new assignment.

Financial Compensation

Be sure the military member gets all the information straight regarding en route compensation available for family members. Because we're such a large family, and because we can be economical on the road, there was one move where we would actually make three hundred dollars more if we took ten days to reach our destination rather than trying to make it in seven. Compensation varies greatly according to a variety of factors, so be sure you understand these matters before you hit the road.

Use It or Lose It

There are certain items that movers are not allowed to transport. The reason is obvious for flammables, aerosol cans, and opened products. So use all these items up as well as you can (i.e., don't buy extra gas for the lawn mower if you're just going to have to drain the tank before you move it; the same would apply to propane for your barbeque grill).

Also plan a strategy for using up food in the freezer and refrigerator. The month before your move, take inventory of perishable items that you cannot move and make out menus accordingly. Usually glass jars cannot be transported, so keep pantry items in mind as you plan menus as well.

You might even want to have a party if you just bought a side of beef and your assignment orders came two weeks later!

Stuff and Cram

Even if you don't do a complete DITY, what you take with you as "essentials" qualifies for compensation if you are not over your weight allowance. For example, Bob is allowed twenty thousand pounds (give or take a thousand), and the last trip we hauled four thousand pounds (including a full travel trailer) of essentials for our family. The movers hauled seventeen thousand pounds, so we were compensated for three thousand pounds of the weight we hauled with us. But remember not to take more than you can carry! We've learned that the hard way: as I kept bringing stuff out to Bob to "pack" for our last move, he got to the point where we didn't have room for one of the kids because he'd accidentally packed his seat full of stuff!

Prepacking Tips From the Experts

Videotape

Karen Evensen, a former USAF wife, says, "Videotape the contents of your house before you pack your belongings. This is not only good for insurance purposes but also for redecorating—so you can remember what kind of arrangement you had in the rooms of your previous home. If there is ever any question as to the quantity, condition, or value of an item, you have the proof. It is also helpful if you don't have time to do a detailed inventory of books and small items. Just make sure to tape slowly and close up. And speaking of small items, put the TV remotes in plastic bags and tape them directly to the TV."

Utensils and Small Items

"Put all your silverware and other utensils in gallon-size zip-lock bags. That way they stay clean, and you don't have to wash them when you get to your destination. They go right into the drawer," says Jill Mingear, wife of an Army helicopter pilot. She adds, "Use two-gallon-size bags for toys with many parts or for games. Use one of these bags for screws, bolts, and nuts for the larger pieces of furniture, such as beds. Tape these bags to a drawer or the back of the furniture."

Sheets

Bonnie Weida, an Air Force wife, says, "Put clean sheets in a plastic bag and zip them into the mattress before a move. This makes them easy to find without going through boxes."

Trash and Treasure

"Empty all your trash cans and wash them out before they are moved. Movers will even box up the garbage!" says Jody Dale, USA wife and mother of three. She adds, "Keep the kids' audio- and videotapes and books out for traveling and put them in a neighbor's home for the day. The movers can pack so quickly that these 'travel necessities' could find themselves inside the moving van rather than your minivan!"

Pets

Karen Evensen also says, "If you have a cat, get the disposable-type kitty litter box for while you're moving and setting up your new household. They also fit on the floor of the car or under the seat in a van and can be covered up when not in use. They usually don't smell, and when you are done with your move, the entire box goes into the trash."

Many pets can get in the packers' way and even harm themselves. Consider putting them in a neighbor's yard or kennel for the big day. Ask your veterinarian for sleeping or travel sickness pills to help your pet sleep during travel days. Think about your pet's safety and comfort as you travel and plan accordingly. For example, be sure an animal is never left in the car on hot days. Be sure that your pet's tags have current and accurate information printed on them. For example, if you move from New Mexico to Germany and your pet gets lost in Illinois, the "finder" needs the phone number of a relative or veterinarian who knows where you are!

Survival Box

Karen also recommends making a "survival box." She makes sure it is the last item ON the truck and the first one OFF. It should contain toilet paper, Kleenex, an iron, towels, bedding, and a shower curtain.

Children

Young children should be in the care of a family member or neighbor on moving day to ensure their safety. However, it's important that they see part of moving day so they know their stuff didn't just disappear—it went into a box and is on the way to the new home!

Packing Day

On the day the packers arrive, be prepared. Know how many packers will come and how much they plan to accomplish that day. If they do not show up on time, have too few workers, or stop working excessively early, call the representative from the relocation office or TMO (Traffic

Management Office). If you have a friend (or two) who has offered to help you on that day, have him/her stay in a room where packers are working while you are with other packers.

Ask for *standup wardrobe boxes,* where you can hang your clothing on hangers. Not only do the lay-down boxes wrinkle clothing more easily, you have to re-hang perhaps hundreds of items. If you have a special collectible, such as an antique clock or fragile figurine, ask the packers to create a *custom packing box* for that item with extra packing inside.

Mark It! and Bless 'Em!

Cindy Musselwhite, an Army spouse, says, "Make sure the boxes are marked appropriately. I was once six months pregnant when we moved and thought we had all the boxes marked 'clothes' sent to our temporary quarters. My maternity clothes never arrived, and I finally had to break down and buy more. When we got on post, I was eight months pregnant, and we finally found the clothes in a box marked 'garden hoses.'"

Jody Dale, an Army chaplain's wife, offers this perspective: Take good care of your packers. She says, "Carry a magic marker and put specific labels on the boxes. It will make for a less hectic unpacking day. Put all the clothes and personal items that you're taking with you in your car or put them in a neighbor's house." Jody adds, "We bless the movers/packers with food, kindness, and laughter. We believe many people pick on them and abuse them, giving them a hard time due to past experiences. But we have had some great guys and gals respond to our kindness by being extra careful with our stuff."

The morning they arrive, let the crew know you're buying pizza for lunch and ask them what kind of soda they like. These are small offers of thoughtfulness, but they mean a lot. It can also mean the difference between the packers *throwing* your stuff in a box versus carefully *packing* your prized possessions!

En Route

It's very common for families who are relocating to want to visit extended family members and friends as they travel from point A to point B. It's important, however, to remember that this is a stressful time, when you may not be at your personal best! Moving is one of the top ten stress factors families face, and the added stress of a military move can make it even harder. Carefully consider who you are going to visit and how much time you will be adding to an already challenging road trip. Have your extended family and friends read this section of the book so they will know that you are under considerable stress, and your entire nuclear family may not be operating at their peak in terms of propriety and thoughtfulness. An extra special amount of grace is required when hosting a family en route.

Another good rule of thumb is that you travel no more than the daily allowed miles for *per diem* compensation. These mileage numbers are usually lower than what "conquer the road at any cost" types will like. However, it's critical that you think of your kids and spouse in this big adventure. Map out your hotel route and search the Internet for ones with pools and free breakfast buffets. Plan to leave after a good breakfast and arrive at the next destination early enough to enjoy the swimming pool and rest up for the next day.

Once You Arrive

Jody Dale says, "Label each room in the house with a number so you can simply tell the movers to put it in room #3. Know exactly where you want large pieces of furniture placed and assembled—especially the beds. I've even marked off these areas in a room with masking tape."

Personally, I believe that moving is a surefire way of determining whether you own your things—or they own you! I was so upset when the movers broke the delicate leg of my grandma's antique cherrywood side table—it made my stomach hurt! It's best to expect some things to be broken and realize that we can either get it fixed or we can't. Being upset for months or years is only going to give us an ulcer!

Be Patient

It's important to realize that Rome wasn't built in a day, and your new home won't be put together in one day either! Pick one room at a time and concentrate on getting it squared away. Play some upbeat, energizing music. Grab a mop, sing along, and keep in step. Your kids will think you've lost your mind, but they will also get a much-deserved laugh after a big transition.

Get Help

Have the movers put together the beds the first night and then have them come back again to unpack boxes—if you want their help. We usually dismiss them that first day, but I've had friends who schedule them back in three days just to unpack the knickknacks that go into curio cases: it takes her many hours to do what two packers and she can do in one hour.

If you have kids, put them in charge of unpacking their own rooms, giving them only as much responsibility as their ages dictate—anything else will only lead to frustration on your part and theirs.

If your sponsor or new neighbor offers to make you dinner—accept! You can return the favor when they make a future move and need a meal while staying in temporary housing.

Even if your children will not be enrolled in base daycare on a regular basis, consider letting them go for the first few days when your house is a complete wreck. They will see more of the home they remember each night when they come home from childcare, and they'll get to play with new friends while you work at home.

If your new lawn needs immediate attention and your equipment is in the bottom of a box, who knows where, ask your neighbors if they know of a teen who does yard work. Even if you don't employ yard care regularly, this one-time job will be worth the expense, as it relieves the pressure of getting the job done right away.

If you're living on base and notice things in your new home that are in need of repair, report them immediately. The same would apply if you're renting a civilian dwelling or apartment; get the landlord to make things right as soon as possible. It will cut down on additional nitpicky stressors!

Unpack It!

Cindy Musselwhite says, "Unpack alongside your packers. We didn't have the packers stay in the same room, and we had a brand-new electric train stolen because of this. We didn't unpack all our boxes at the next assignment, and therefore we didn't discover the theft in time to get reimbursement for the loss."

Treat Yourself!

Capt. Karen Eckerle, USAF, says, "I find the transit part of moving more tolerable by packing comfy slippers for the trip and a fluffy neck pillow (sprayed with a lilac scent). I bring along a candle for the hotel room, a fave comfy blankie (lightweight wool, fleece, or cotton throw) and bubble bath or salts for bath time. I also do A.M./P.M. overall stretches and drink LOTS of water."

When it comes to the other end of moving—unpacking—try playing positive mind games. Set goals, and once you achieve them, treat yourself to something special. For example, if you want to get the dishes and cookware unpacked and put away in your kitchen, once you've done this, treat yourself to a cup of coffee at the neighborhood Starbucks and go by the garden store to pick up a flowering plant for the kitchen. Once you've organized the pantry, buy a new color of nail polish or a magazine that looks interesting and relaxing. After you've got one of the bathrooms completely finished (walls and everything), buy a new scented candle and a bottle of bubble bath and take a long, hot bath!

Join the base's aerobics class or take a walk once a day. It will relieve stress and give you a chance to meet your new neighbors. At the halfway point of your unpacking, go out and get a pedicure, and once the house is completely done, get a manicure at the base beauty salon. If you had one *before* your work was done, you'd only ruin it.

Consider getting a totally new hairstyle when you arrive someplace new. If it turns out really "different," your new friends won't know how good you used to look, and you'll only look better as it grows out!

Treat yourself by treating your house. While it's important to stick to a budget, now is the time to add new color to your living room with a throw and pillows or a new wallpaper border. These modest, low-cost changes are also the splurge you need as you transition to your new home. Arrange the furniture differently than it was in your last home.

One a Day

Once you've gotten your home somewhat settled, only do one errand a day. If you're going to wait a couple of hours to get a new driver's license, don't wait two more hours to get your car plates on the same day! Do your grocery shopping on one day and enroll the kids in school on another.

Family Fun

Make a ceremony with your kids of putting out the welcome mat. Tell them that it is the first thing you put out and the last thing you pack up when you move, because a home should always welcome new and old friends no matter how many times you move.

Make time for scheduled breaks with your kids. Get a good book and take the kids to the park. Take them to the base pool and let them wear themselves out while you sun yourself by the baby pool. After they've finished arranging their shelves of toys or books in their rooms, take them out for a hot-fudge sundae!

Take Notes

Buy a fresh spiral notebook that will fit into your purse or pocket. When someone recommends a baby-sitter, barber, hairstylist, cleaners, or restaurant, take notes with addresses and phone numbers. Write down the names of your neighbors and their house numbers so you know who lives where. Jot down your unit's welcome representative and their phone number. Have your kids add the names of their new friends to your notebook and where they live, then make a note to introduce yourself to their parents if they don't come over to see you first.

Karen Evensen says, "Use sheets or fabric to decorate walls instead of painting or wallpapering. Just put it on with starch. It strips off easily when you need to move again, and you can take it to your next home, plus there is no repainting or wallpaper to strip if you live in base housing. This is especially great for young children, because it helps their rooms seem familiar as they move from house to house."

As you walk from room to room, write down a list of things you'll need for each room; since you're keeping this with you, you'll have it when you need it in the store later. Tape fabric swatches, paint chips, or wallpaper samples to a page in your notebook so you can find a good sale on accessories, such as curtains, valances, and bedding.

Make a list of things you need to do in your new place: call the Welcome Wagon (for discounts, freebies, and leads); call the Chamber of Commerce to send you a packet of information; check your insurance policies; get a driver's license and plates; get a new library card; subscribe to the local newspaper (ask for new customer discounts); find a church; introduce yourself to your mail carrier; make out a list of emergency numbers.

Ways to Make New Friends and Get Used to Your New Home

Get the Thursday paper and a good map and hit the garage sales on Friday and Saturday. You'll familiarize yourself with the neighborhood and make new friends at the same time (unless you ask them if they'll take less for that toaster).

If you have a home business, host a party, or host one for someone else who has a home business. Check out the local MOPS (Mothers of Preschoolers) group if you qualify for this age bracket. Call 1-800-929-1287 or e-mail *info@mops.org* to find a group near you. Join a "Moms in Touch" at your school (go to *www.momsintouch.org* for a group near you). Have your own "Open House" and invite all your neighbors. One friend with a great sense of humor taped a new sign over the "For Sale/ Sold" sign in her front yard. It read: "Wanted: New friend with a short memory and a long sense of humor." She found her new best friend this way!

★   ★   ★

For many couples, their major goal in moving is to stay married. . . .
I know that moving can rank right up there on the "fun things to
experience" list along with wallpapering, root canals, pet-sitting a pit
bull, and having your twelve-month-old triplets all start to teethe at
the same time.
    —JOHN TRENT
        from the foreword of *After the Boxes Are Unpacked*
        by Susan Miller

★ PROFILE ★

Name: Brenda Taylor

Spouse's Name: Maj. Drew Taylor

Branch of Service: USAF

Kids: Lauren and Jonathan

Number of Moves: 6

Years in Service: 16

Work: independent distributor with Premier Designs High Fashion Jewelry

Hobbies: inductive Bible study, exercising, photo albums, singing

Least Favorite Aspect of Military Life: leaving church and friends behind when moving

Favorite Aspect of Military Life: getting to see so much of our great country and the world

CHAPTER SIX

Hidden Hero Portrait—
Brenda Taylor

Gorgeous in Guam and Happy in Hawaii

~

Military life has a way of drawing courage out of the timid and an adventurous spirit out of those with deep roots, and that is what happened in Brenda's case. "I was not yet twenty when I married my Air Force husband," says soft-spoken Brenda in a slight southern drawl as she puts strands of her long brown hair behind her ear and smiles shyly. "My family wondered if it would work out, especially since we were moving to Guam immediately after the wedding."

The couple honeymooned in Hawaii en route to the island of Guam, their sunny paradise for the next two years. Brenda noticed that her husband, Drew, seemed to have so much fun flying the B-52 that she decided she'd get in on the action too and applied for a job as a flight attendant with Continental Air Micronesia.

Tall and slender, Brenda donned the uniform of her new job: a pink and white floral *muumuu* that was fitted with a long straight skirt with slits on both sides. She looked gorgeous and was an immediate favorite among the passengers who flew her routes. She went from sunny Florida to the skyways of Bali, Indonesia; Sydney, Australia; Manila, Philippines; Tokyo, Japan; Honolulu, Hawaii; and even one memorable trip to Papua New Guinea.

Brenda looked at her work as mainly a day job: "I flew out in the morning and was home in time for dinner. I traded off overnight trips with other flight attendants so I could be home with my husband in the evenings. But sometimes I wasn't able to trade off a trip." That's how she was in a position to have her one and only trip to the outer regions of civilization in New Guinea.

Even though Brenda was making great strides in her independence, she still preferred to spend her nights at home as a newlywed with her husband. For a full year she managed to strategically trade off her trips and avoid as many layovers as possible, but every now and then she would be required to have a layover. In fact, she managed to have a layover in Hawaii about once every two months in order to shop! As she served refreshments to the passengers, she thought of their destination and what lay ahead. She tried not to think about the strange hotel, the unusual culture of the people there, and the fact that she would be alone in a place she'd never been before. Instead, she looked over the passengers in the seating area. They were flying a 727 designed to carry one-half cargo and one-half passengers. The crew fondly called these specially configured jets "NuJu" and "JuJu."

As the airline made its final approach to the narrow airstrip in Papua New Guinea, Brenda buckled into her flight attendant's seat and looked out the window. She described it as "always amazing to me how we'd approach the island from the ocean and then the runway would appear, looking like a postage stamp from the air." She saw what looked like a fenced field on either side of the primitive runway, but the most amazing thing was that it looked like there were crowds of people pressing against the fences, their tiny figures distinguishable even from the airplane's landing altitude. But she had no idea what these people looked like until the plane landed.

Brenda was surprised at what she saw when the jet turned and headed toward the "terminal" buildings in this exotic land. The people she viewed from inside the 727 were clearly visible from the window. They were half-naked with tattooed, exotic faces, their bare bodies an expression of their culture.

As Brenda disembarked after the passengers, the wind took her (and her muumuu) by surprise. The people crowded the fences to get a closer look at the Western world. Brenda said, "We felt like animals in a zoo exhibit as they crowded to see what Westerners looked like." At the time, all Brenda could think of was a National Geographic documentary about the cannibalistic customs of primitive tribal villages in the region.

She looked at the faces and thought, Cannibals? No, I won't even THINK about that!

She began to hear a chant going up among one of the groups of people huddled together by the fence, and she stole another side-glance at them.

They were smiling at her and nodding their heads enthusiastically.

And they looked hungry.

Very hungry.

★　★　★

The dilapidated hotel bus drove her to a typical hotel on the island. As the vehicle bumped down the dirt road, she tried to talk herself out of the apprehension she felt for the unknown. She reasoned: *I have no other choice; I'm not a child. I've had layovers before. I'm a professional, and this is part of my new job. Other flight attendants make this stopover all the time. I know I've never been here before, but I've survived a lot of new experiences in the past year, and I know I can do this.*

The ancient clerk at the desk, dressed in a brightly colored Hawaiian-print shirt with khaki pants, appeared to be somewhat preoccupied with the organization of a ring of room keys he was sorting. He smiled a wary grin at Brenda but managed to understand her well enough to assign her a room.

Brenda tried the lock on her door, and it seemed to be stable enough. The room was much larger than she'd ever had before and was neat and clean. She closed the door behind her and locked it. There was a rickety chain on the door that looked as if it would give out at the slightest pressure, but she hooked it to the doorframe for added security. She noticed a phone on the nightstand and thought, *At least I can call Drew if I get scared—it would only take him ten hours to get here.*

She pulled out her Bible and read her favorite Psalm that always seemed to calm her when she faced something new and different—in fact, she'd read it often since marrying her Air Force husband. All the tension finally caught up with her as she fell asleep, completely spent emotionally and physically from the long flight.

Suddenly she was wide awake.

There was a noise at the door!

Jolted from her deep sleep, she sat straight up in bed and struggled to remember where she was and why she had such a fearful feeling inside. She swiftly glanced around the room, her eyes focusing on the digital clock: 2:30 A.M.

The door rattled a second time.

Then someone fit a key into the lock and began to open the door.

From somewhere deep within, she discovered a newfound courage and shouted, "What are you doing here? This room is occupied!"

Her demand was answered by a voice that replied in broken English, "Dey give key to dis room at desk. So sorry."

It turned out the distracted clerk had booked the room twice!

She never returned to Papua New Guinea. (But she *did* go back to Hawaii!)

That was fifteen years and six assignments ago. Today Brenda is a veteran hero on the home front, having completed her college degree as a military spouse. She taught first grade, started a home business as an independent jeweler for Premier, and has two children. She's lived in Minot, North Dakota, where the snow piled higher than her house. She's also lived in Columbus, Mississippi, where the heat and humidity are so bad in the summer, you must run your errands before nine in the morning or you will be in a steam bath.

This may not seem remarkable on the surface, but think about it. . . . Brenda, at the age of nineteen, when most kids are in college and going home on weekends to give their mom their laundry, decided to take a chance and marry a military man. She left her comfortable roots and not only had to start a new life with her husband (which ranks right up there on the stress charts) but she also had to adjust to a new culture, a dramatic job change (from waitress to Asian stewardess), and the other difficulties of military life. Through it all, Brenda has clung to two things: her faith and her family. She says, "I'm thankful to be a military spouse. The friends made, areas explored, and experiences gained have been well worth the sacrifice of leaving 'home'!"

Brenda is not alone . . . hundreds of military spouses like her, like you, leave what they know to follow who they love. That's pretty remarkable. No wonder they call you a hero.

Brenda's Psalm

> You who live in the shelter of the Most High,
> who abide in the shadow of the Almighty,
> will say to the Lord,
> "My refuge and my fortress;
> my God, in whom I trust."
> For he will deliver you from
> the snare of the fowler
> and from the deadly pestilence;
> he will cover you with his pinions,
> and under his wings you will find refuge;
> his faithfulness is a shield and buckler.
> You will not fear the terror of the night.
> —Psalm 91 NRSV

Celebrating
Laughter

CHAPTER SEVEN

Rent a Yenta
Using Humor to Lighten the Load

⌒

My husband was off flying a jet somewhere over the Middle East during the last days of Desert Storm. I was back home managing a storm of my own: a three-year-old, an eighteen-month-old, and a newborn. To win the war I would battle this morning, I knew I had to have my troops up by sunrise—for I had discovered the best time to attack the grocery store is by dawn's early light.

If you have never been to the grocery store before seven in the morning, I highly recommend it. Meeting interesting characters makes it worth the extra effort. I do need to offer a small warning to mothers of multiple pre-schoolers, however. Early shoppers don't usually have children at home, and I've found they love nothing more than helping out mothers with a cartful of kids.

On this particular morning, I drove to the store, stuffed my three kids in the cart, and pushed my basket of kids-on-wheels up and down the aisles while pulling another cart full of groceries. This was no easy operation. All I wanted to do was garner the strength to finish my mule-like task and hoof it out of the store!

As I rounded the corner near an Oreo cookie display, I nearly ran over a Yenta. Yes, Yenta. As in "little matchmaker" from Fiddler on the Roof? She wore her gray hair wrapped in a scarf, and, in spite of her thick New York accent, she even sounded like Yenta.

"Oh, my goodness; oh, my gosh!" the woman exclaimed, smacking her forehead with her open palm as she carried on a conversation with herself.

"I can't believe what I see heyah!" She pointed at me but directed her question to herself. "Can you believe this?" I wondered if she was about to respond to herself.

Yenta squinted in deep concern, patting my arm as she spoke. "Can you believe this? Did you knowah that you could put yah back out doing that?" Turning, she quizzed her alter ego: "Can she put her back out or what? Pulling and pushing those carts full of food and kids?"

For once, I was speechless. No matter—my newfound mentor was quick to fill in the silence. "You could put yah back out, that's what. They have people heah that can push those carts for ya." She spied a stock boy unloading boxes in the dairy section and shouted, "Hey, youwah! Yeah, you, mistah! I don't mean ya mutha', I don't mean ya fatha', I mean YOUWAH! COME HEYAH, NOW!"

The startled stock boy came running as she scolded him. "Did yah know that this woman is going to put her back out?" Turning again, she asked her invisible friend, "Is she going to put her back out or what?" Looking back to the bewildered teenager, she stomped her foot. "Yes, she's going to put her back out, and where will ya be then, I ASK YOU? You'll be in the poorhouse, that's what. She'll put her back out, sue your store, and you'll be out of a job, that's what. So ya'd bettah push her cart to the check-out, and ya'd bettah do it NOW!"

Not wanting to lose his job or take on a lawsuit, the boy immediately went to work pushing my cart of groceries. Overwhelmed by the entire experience, I stared at Yenta, opened my mouth to say something, and again, nothing came out.

She helped me. "I know what you ah thinking . . . Yes, I know what you ah thinking. Do we know"—she turned—"what she's thinking?"

She struck the pose of a saint, one hand gently resting in the palm of the other. "You ah thinking that ya'd like to say thank you. No need to say it; I do things like this because I love people. A poor widow woman alone in de world, but I'm always thinking of others. Yes, I love people, that's what." As she walked away, I could faintly hear her asking, "Do we love people or what? I ask you . . ."

★ ★ ★

Jerry Lewis once said, "There are three things that are real: God, human folly, and laughter. Since the first two are beyond our comprehension, we must do what we can with the third." This lesson is a must for all families, military or civilian. Sometimes we have to step back and see the humor in the seriousness of life. In some cases, it may take months or years to crack a smile at an incident that happened while our loved one was away on deployment or even at war—as in my case above.

Humor isn't the only way to beat the stress; there are a wide variety of methods that individuals and families use to beat the heat. But humor is an easy and usually safe way to take the high road out of an argument, a bad mood, or a tension-filled room. Laughter is healthy for us. Studies show that those who laugh—last. Yes, they live longer.

Having an understanding of human beings and becoming a student of their behavior will always give us something to grin about. That's why understanding and humor often walk hand in hand. Some of the wisest guys I know are the ones who make me laugh the most. They're the ones I want beside me when Bob's flying far away or when my writing deadlines are about to bury me.

As you read through the ways various people, families, and organizations cope using humor and understanding, try to think of the stories you would add to this list—and mail them to me. Or mail them to *Reader's Digest*'s "Humor in Uniform" for a $300 payment and the chance to be published! Who says humor doesn't pay?

Here are a few of my favorites, many of them submitted by people just like you!

How About Them Yankees?

Just this past year, Bob and I learned just how much humor can cut marital tension. We were in a marriage communication class and learned that when we find ourselves arguing about the issues of life, we could develop a code phrase that essentially means, "Are we making a mountain out of a mole hill?" It's a reality check for both parties, and it's not meant to be a slam on our partner. We decided that our code phrase would be "How about them Yankees?" When one of us said this, we would realize that we were probably sweating the small stuff, and it would cut the tension. We chose the phrase because the Yankees were playing in the World Series at the time and doing some amazing things.

We have found it works surprisingly well. Here's an example:

Bob: "Hey, Beloved, did you notice I washed your Suburban?"

Ellie: "Really? Then why is it muddy; I noticed it when I dropped off the kids at school."

Bob: (Running out to the garage while Ellie follows) "WHAT? I just spent two hours detailing this YESTERDAY and it's all mud-splattered! Plus, you didn't even notice that it was clean right after I did all that work!"

Ellie: "Gosh! I'm running around after these kids; how COULD I notice? I wonder how it got muddy?"

Bob: "Did you take the construction route to school again this morning?"

Ellie: "Yeah, I did, and I guess it was kind of muddy where they hosed down the dirt they're working on. Hey! I can't help it if the road is muddy!"

Bob: "You could have taken it real slow, because the car WAS clean!"

Ellie: "How am I suppose to know the car is clean unless you tell me! Besides that, the speed limit in that area is only 15 miles per hour; how much slower am I suppose to go?!"

Bob: "How about them Yankees?"

Male/Female Differences

After the bestselling Mars/Venus phenomenon, a slew of books on the differences between men and women flooded the market. These issues can lead to great conflict unless we learn to celebrate the differences between men and women. One of the best ways to do this is to look at these relational dynamics in a lighthearted way.

One of the best books on male/female differences is by my friends Bill and Pam Farrel, entitled *Men Are Like Waffles—Women Are Like Spaghetti* (Harvest House, 2001). I heard Pam give the following speech to a room full of pastors. Enjoy:

If She Says	**She Really Means**
We need.	I want.
It's your decision.	The correct decision should be obvious.
Do what you want.	You'll pay for this later.
You're . . . so manly.	You need a shave and you sweat a lot.
This kitchen is so inconvenient.	I want a new house.
You have to learn to communicate.	Just agree with me.
I'm sorry.	You'll be sorry.
You're certainly attentive tonight.	Is sex all you ever think about?

If He Says	**He Really Means**
I'm hungry.	I'm hungry.
I'm sleepy.	I'm sleepy.

I'm tired.	I'm tired.
Do you want to go to a movie?	I'd eventually like to have sex with you.
Can I take you out to dinner?	I'd eventually like to have sex with you.
What's wrong? (first time)	I don't see why you're making such a big deal about this.
What's wrong? (second time)	What meaningless, self-inflicted psychological trauma are you going through now?
What's wrong? (third time)	I guess sex tonight is out of the question.

The point of this section and books that deal with these issues is that men and women communicate differently. We have a basic choice: We can learn the other person's language and celebrate the difference, or we can continue to fight World War III.

Pass the Rolls, Please!

Sometimes our family gets so busy with hectic schedules and the drag of the daily grind that we find ourselves rarely laughing. At times the desire to lighten up is a deliberate, thoughtful choice. Other times it's spontaneous. Still others, it's both.

For example, one month we'd been going nonstop, the pressure of a deadline was upon me, and Bob was getting ready for a huge inspection. Life was tough. Life was tense. We needed a respite.

As we sat at the dinner table one night, I looked over the heads of our five children, whom we had been correcting throughout the meal. We are real sticklers on table manners, and this sticks in their craw at times. The kids were kind of exhausted from the constant correction as they sat up straight, napkins in lap, and closed mouths while chewing. I asked Bob to pass the rolls.

"Sure!" he said cheerfully.

Then he took a roll from the basket and *threw* it at me, the full length of the eight-foot table! I raised my right hand, caught it mid-air, and went back to eating my peas. The kids "rolled" in laughter, and our momentary burdens were lifted. That's what it means to lighten up.

That's Not Funny!

Rodney Dangerfield has become famous for his one-liners about how he can never get any respect. His wife seems to be the primary target of many of these "lack of respect" jokes. For example, Rodney says, "I call my wife to tell her I got hit by a bus on the way home from work, and she says, 'I guess this means I'll have to walk the dog.' "

There are certain things that are funny, and others just aren't. No matter how many years pass by and no matter what new spin you put on a problem, some things will never be funny. A good rule of thumb regarding what is worth joking about and what is not, is this: Does it violate the other person's line of respect?

A line of respect is a boundary that leaves the other person's self-esteem intact. If your humor attacks the *person* rather than the *action,* it will usually violate a line of respect. Men and women don't seem to merely *want* respect from their spouse, we actually *need* it to feel that we are important and that what we do matters. This isn't the same as feeding each other's ego. We are talking about genuine praise for actions, attitudes, and character traits that you admire in your mate. *Tell him* about the things you appreciate. This means that when friends at a Christmas party start to "joke" about their spouses by ridiculing them verbally and publicly, you will refrain. Some jokes just aren't funny—they're hurtful and are really daggers cloaked in "humor."

Bob and I made a commitment to each other the first month we were married: We would never make a joke at the other's expense, either in public or private. It's been hard to keep that commitment, especially among fighter pilots who delight in making themselves feel important by cutting the other guy down. One of their favorite lines was "You are so pretty; how did you get stuck with a guy like Bob?" Then they would laugh at their wit and be very pleased with themselves. If I laughed and said nothing, it would seem as if I agreed. So I said, "Are you kidding? I got the better end of the deal: I married the World's Greatest Fighter Pilot!" Not only did it shut those guys up, it gave me my favorite saying that I still use today.

Humor From All Branches of the Service

Oh, My! Semper Fi!

Military families aren't the only ones who benefit from lightening up in appropriate settings; active duty members are notorious for their antics—some are legendary. It's so much fun to recount these stories to each other and to find laughter and release each time we hear them. Tom Neven, a former Marine, is currently the editor of *Focus on the Family Magazine.* He tells the story of when he was stationed in Okinawa at

Camp Hansen with the First Battalion, Fourth Marines. Someone broke into the provost marshal's office, where they had an audiotape player that broadcast the national anthem and "Marines' Hymn" at 0800 every morning. The "criminal" substituted a Led Zeppelin tape. At 0800 the next morning, as each unit was waiting to raise the morning colors, a raucous "Whole Lotta Love" blasted across the base instead!

McRivalries—Aim High!

After 9/11, when military units were awaiting orders to deploy, tensions were understandably high. At Holloman Air Force Base, two rival squadrons found an acceptable (if unconventional) way to cut the pressure through a series of practical jokes. It started when the 8th Fighter Squadron "borrowed" the mascot of the 9th Fighter Squadron—the Knight. They took it all around town and took pictures of it in front of "The Tin Man Smoke Shop," in the toy train at the zoo, at the grocery store, and even in front of a sign for an adult bookstore. Then they sent a ransom note and the photos to the squadron.

As if that weren't enough, a few months later the 8th Fighter Squadron was at it again. They stole the 9th Fighter Squadron's flag. In its place, in broad daylight, they managed to sneak in and raise none other than—the McDonald's flag. They took a digital photo of the flag flying proudly in front of the 9th Fighter Squadron and e-mailed the operations desk with an attachment of the photo. It was their way of alerting their rival to their treachery—the photo had text superimposed over it that read: "You want fries with that?"

Going a Little Batty

Civil Service employee Farrell Morton, of the Det 182 Aerial Targets Squadron, says she had decorated their office for Halloween with all the typical fare, and the area was appropriately adorned for the holidays. The colonel's wife and daughter decided that his office was drab by comparison, so after hours they decorated it and closed the door. The next morning he was greeted with a beautiful frilly confection of his least favorite colors and toys: pink and Barbie. It seems he had an intense dislike for Pepto-Bismol pink and was always tripping over Barbies at home.

Parade Colors—The Army Keeps Rolling Along

It was Col. Bill Caldwell's change of command ceremony, in which he gave up his brigade to his successor. This commander was much loved by his men and women in the 10th Mountain Division in Fort Drum,

New York. They would follow him into any battle anytime, anyplace, anywhere. During the customary parade in which the marching band performed, we noticed a tuba player in the back that was marching a little irregularly. Whispers started like waves among the crowd; finally the ripple met our ears and mixed with waves of laughter as we realized that the colonel's personnel officer, Lt. Col. Marty Klein, had confiscated a tuba and was marching with the band as a tribute to his commander. Afterward he said, "I wanted to do something special for a special man, and I thought this would make it memorable and fun for everyone." He didn't know how to play the tuba, but he never missed a beat.

Navy Sea Bats

Tom Neven, a former Marine, tells the story of his first time aboard a Navy ship. The sailors told the new Marines that they had just captured a sea bat—a rare find. It was contained in an upside-down fifty-gallon drum. In order for the Marines to see the bat, the sailors had them get down on their hands and knees while another sailor gently tipped the barrel. They were cautioned to not let the sea bat fly out the bottom when the drum was tipped. In this position, the Marine's posterior was elevated, and when the timing was just right—WHAM! A sailor walloped the man on his backside.

Tom said it took one of his fellow Marines *three times* to finally catch on to the prank. The Marine got down on his hands and knees, and each time he got hit with the broom, he'd turn and say in a frustrated voice, "Hey! Stop it! I'm trying to see the sea bat!"

Language Barrier—English Versus English

Kris King, married to MSgt. Ben King, was stationed in England and quickly learned that American English and the King's English are not the same. Her husband was working in civil engineering at the time, and she went into the office to explain a problem she was having with her hot-water tank. After a few moments one of the British repairmen replied, "No problem, mum, I'll fix your problem. I'll come knock you up at eight tomorrow morning!" She stood there stunned and speechless for what seemed like an eternity, until he explained that "knock you up" means to knock on your door and wake you up!

★   ★   ★

So the next time you've just been told you're moving in two weeks, or any variety of stressors that are unique to the military, think about ways you can help your family lighten up through the use of appropriate humor. It's a healing balm with amazing power.

CHAPTER EIGHT

Queen of Everything

Stress Busters

~

*E*very year at Holloman Air Force Base, two flying squadrons bring out
a dozen sleek black F-117A fighters and set them out on the flight line ramp.
The area between two sets of specially designed hangars that house the F-
117s is called "The Canyon." The pilots' wives were going to have their
annual photo shoot in front of these awesome jets—and it was no laughing
matter. These women took this photo-op very seriously, and I was about to
discover just how serious. We were instructed to wear white T-shirts, blue
jeans, black boots, and brown bomber jackets (borrowed from our hubbies).
We dubbed ourselves the Blue-Jeaned Stealth Queens as we strutted our stuff
in front of the jets. Never mind the fact that all together we had 48 kids, 187
loads of laundry, and 67 dogs waiting for us at home. We were proud that
we still had "it." The only problem was—most of us couldn't remember
where we put it.

I was excited about being a Stealth Queen. Hey, I'd been called the
"Coupon Queen" and the "Savings Queen" for years—why couldn't I just
be Queen of Everything? So I thought royalty could slide on the dress code a
bit: instead of the mandatory white T-shirt, I had an ecru-colored shirt on.
I thought the jacket would cover it and no one would notice. I was wrong.

When we were ready to walk out with the photographer, a mean-eyed
mama thrust a white T-shirt under my nose and hissed, "Quick, put this
on; that ecru-colored shirt will ruin the overall effect."

Now is a good time to mention an important fact about a certain limitation I have. You see, when God passed out common sense, he gave my
friend Myra a double portion and reduced my part to a morsel.

So I stood there looking at the guys on the flight line. The entire crew *was resting in the shade by the jets. There were no bathrooms nearby, and the mean-eyed mama was staring at me with her lips tensed, tapping her foot. How in the world was I going to take off my ecru shirt and change into the white T-shirt in front of God and country and mechanics?*

My thoughts were interrupted by a tap on my shoulder. It was common-sensed Myra. "Ellie, you could just slip the white T-shirt over the shirt you're wearing now," she said.

"Uh, yes, uh, of course," I stammered, wondering why I hadn't thought of the obvious.

I quickly pulled on the white T-shirt and then found myself faced with yet another problem. You see, when a woman has had a basketball team's worth of children, there's a basic problem. I was wearing "Great Shapes" No Nonsense panty hose (they guarantee to take five pounds off any figure). In fact, I was wearing two pair to remove that extra ten pounds.

There was no way I could leave that shirt untucked, or the added bulk would make me look like a buffalo in that there canyon. Once again my hero, Myra, came to my rescue. "Here, Ellie, Marcie and I will hold up our jackets while you tuck your shirt in."

What a relief!

The two women held up their jackets, shielding the view from the flight-crew members by the jets.

I quickly dropped my pants low enough to neatly tuck in my shirt and pulled them up again. With a sigh of relief, I zipped the jeans and turned around to pick up my jacket from the pavement. At that moment I saw an awful sight.

To my utter embarrassment, I noticed, for the first time, a row of twelve men sitting in the shade of the hangar about two hundred yards behind me. The girls shielded the view of the guys in front of us, but no one saw the crowd behind us.

Myra noticed the Peeping Toms at the same time I did and was quick to comfort me with "Hey, Ellie, don't worry about it; I don't think they even noticed."

Momentary relief accompanied my hope that maybe Myra was right and they hadn't noticed. I slowly stole a side-glance at the group sitting in the shade.

They were waving at me, slapping each other on the back—and laughing.

★　★　★

Sometimes I create my own stress. As if it weren't enough that Uncle Sam is constantly trying to check my fortitude with unexpected deployments, bizarre moving scenarios, and remote locations—I contribute to the mix in ignorance or vanity. Yep, I'm "Queen of Scream" when I get caught doing foolish things. It was months before I could think of the Stealth Queen incident without turning beet red. It took even longer for me to actually laugh at it. (To be honest, I still haven't laughed; the best I can do is crack a grin.) It's an incident that keeps me humble when the "Superwoman Syndrome" beckons me to succumb to its impossible standards.

But even if we can't laugh at ourselves, there are scores of other stress-relieving activities that help us in our journey toward joy. Here are a few ideas from the experts:

A Matter of Perspective

De-stressing can, on occasion, be as easy as changing the way you view a challenge. For example: moving. When we've moved to a new area, sometimes it is hard to even think of the positive aspects of a move. Here are some advantages to being the new family on the block. Some of these tips have been adapted from Susan Miller's wonderful book on moving, *After the Boxes Are Unpacked* (Focus on the Family Publishing, 1995).

- You have a completely clean house before you move in.
- You have the opportunity to share some of the stuff you don't need with others who do need it (why not give that high chair to Goodwill?).
- You'll unpack items you can use but forgot you had—thus saving you the expense of buying them again.
- Maybe some of the old clothes you've held on to for twenty years have come back in style! (They probably won't fit you, but they may fit your teenager.)
- You have more control over time, because you don't have old commitments.
- No one in your new neighborhood has seen your wardrobe; it's like getting a new one each time you move!
- You have the opportunity to reprioritize your life.
- Moving will give you a better education by broadening your perspective along with your horizons.
- As Anne of Avonlea said, "Tomorrow is always new, with no mistakes

in it." You have a chance to be known for who you are today and not who you were yesterday.

- All the same old, same old—those things that are old to you about yourself and your family—will be new and exciting to others.

Exercise Your Body—The Natural Stress-Buster

For years medical experts have told us that regular exercise helps lower our cholesterol, increases our metabolism, and helps fight heart disease. Not only can you join an aerobics class, find a walking partner, or swim laps in the base pool, in addition to *individual* exercise, you can encourage your *family* to do some of these things together. Our family started playing racquetball together—there's nothing like whacking that rubber ball against a wall to release some pent-up stress!

Army spouse Jody Dale says, "Our family walks a lot and enjoys hiking together for exercise. It really has a calming effect when someone is out of sorts or otherwise stressed. We also play tennis, even though none of us are really that good at it. But that's what makes it fun. We laugh at ourselves and at each other. We have table tennis contests too. We videotape a lot of these contests, and the kids always have fun watching these old home movies. It makes us to remember how time flies, and what really matters is each other and not the stressful circumstances that often surround us."

According to MetLife's consumer education center pamphlet, there are ways to make exercise a habit that work with amazing effectiveness. Here are a few of them:

- Choose an activity you enjoy.
- Tailor your program to your own fitness level.
- Set realistic goals.
- Choose an exercise that fits your lifestyle.
- Give your body a chance to adjust to your new routine.
- Don't get discouraged if you don't see immediate results.
- Don't give up if you miss a day; just get back on track the next day.
- Find a partner for a little motivation and socialization.
- Build some rest days into your exercise schedule.
- Listen to your body. If you have difficulty breathing or experience faintness or prolonged weakness during or after exercise, consult your physician.

Exercise Your Brain

A real key in the lives of those who are the most productive, even into their later years, is the ability to keep their brain cells working. Here is a list of seven ways to accomplish this, taken from *Lists to Live By* (Multnomah Publishers, 1999).

- Play complex puzzles and games such as Scrabble or chess.
- Learn a foreign language.
- Study music.
- Solve math problems without using a calculator.
- Write letters or poetry.
- Engage in thought-provoking discussions.
- Study and memorize Scripture.

Sleep It Off

If you're sleeping all the time, it could be a sign of depression, but how do you know if you're getting enough sleep? The right amount of rest is key to your ability to manage and handle stress. Patricia Anstett wrote the following quiz in *The Oregonian* to help readers know if they're getting enough sleep. If you answer yes to three or more of the fifteen items listed, you are like thousands of Americans who are probably not getting enough sleep.

1. I need an alarm to wake up at the appropriate time.
2. It's a struggle for me to get out of bed in the morning.
3. Weekday mornings I hit the snooze button several times to get more sleep.
4. I feel tired, irritable, and stressed-out during the week.
5. I have trouble concentrating and remembering.
6. I feel slow in critical thinking, problem solving, and being creative.
7. I often fall asleep watching TV.
8. I often fall asleep in meetings, in lectures, or in warm rooms.
9. I often fall asleep after heavy meals or after a low dose of alcohol.
10. I often fall asleep while relaxing after dinner.
11. I often fall asleep within five minutes of getting into bed.
12. I often feel drowsy while driving.
13. I often sleep extra hours on weekend mornings.
14. I often need a nap to get through the day.
15. I have dark circles around my eyes.

The answer to sleep problems seems simple: "Get more sleep." But it goes a little further than that. It's important to keep regular hours, get to bed and wake up at the same time each day, and prioritize your schedule to accommodate this much-needed, stress-relieving practice of sleep therapy.

Bathroom Reading

Cindy Musselwhite says, "We keep funny books in the bathroom. One is a knock-knock book, and the other is a Christian joke book. You know the old saying 'A mother only has time to read in the bathroom,' so make good use of it. Well, I come out smiling every time."

Wendy Wendler, an AF spouse, uses the same room for another kind of reading: "Soak in a warm tub with lavender essential oil added for maximum relaxation. Of course, to maximize the experience, you will want to have a good book to read, a cup of smooth coffee, and some dark chocolate."

Smoothie Contest

Another tip from Jody Dale is to have a shake or smoothie contest. They all take turns in the kitchen creating the "best shake or smoothie." Then they have a taste test to choose the winner, awarding points for "best taste" and the "most creative." The losers have to clean up. She concludes, "The kids love it! We always laugh and sometimes gag tasting those crazy concoctions." (Jody has so many great ideas; I think I want to go live at her house!)

Professional Help

Part of the human condition is that there are times when no method, activity, or technique will fix the stress we're under, and that's when it's time to see a counselor. If you are experiencing the majority of the following danger signals, consider seeing a counselor at the Family Support Center or mental health facility on base/post:

- frequent headaches or stomach pains;
- more negative talk than usual;
- more difficult to laugh than before;
- procrastinating the important to accomplish the unimportant;
- less patient and more irritable than normal;
- feeling one step away from falling apart;
- sleeping problems;
- abuse of non-prescription drugs, alcohol, or food to relax;

- feeling exhausted when awake;
- trouble concentrating;
- easily distracted;
- being forgetful and absentminded.

If the last three items on the list are the only ones that count, any preschool mom would qualify as "dangerously stressed." But if eight or more items listed above describe you and your life, then it's time to consult a trained professional.

Stress Busters for Kids at Special Times

Sometimes the stress of military life (especially a parent's absence) hits our kids hardest, and they deal with it in not-so-special ways. If you have kids in your military family, you can count on at least a few times when their feelings are manifested in a negative way. Here are some tips that can apply to our kids when they come home with a bad grade, get in a fight at school, or develop a mouth that gives new meaning to "back talk."

Be kind. The first inclination is to return evil for evil, but extra patience is needed; just as we need time to adjust, so do they. This is in no way an excuse to condone negative behavior, but we must refrain from returning it in kind.

Pray. Now might be a good time to call the local military chaplain and make an appointment to talk through and pray through this stormy season with your child. But *you* can also pray with your child as you pass along your personal faith.

No Excuses. We don't have to explain our child's behavior to everyone. Only talk to those directly involved in the problem. Don't give your child an excuse to believe that you are gossiping about their behavior. They hear and see more than we give them credit for.

Concentrate on Today. Don't look too far forward or backward, and encourage your child to do the same.

Be Honest. There's a difference between being painfully honest and patiently honest. Let your child know how you feel and stress the "I felt hurt when you said that" rather than the "You hurt me when you said that." Teach your children how to express themselves in this way and it will help them get the tension out in constructive, productive ways that will enhance their communication skills in the future.

Don't Fear. When our kids go through transitions, and we are committed to their growth and to helping them in productive ways, we need to teach them to not fear. For example, Anne Alde, wife of a retired general, said: "When my children were afraid of lightning storms, I told them that God is taking our picture and the angels are bowling."

Get Help. If your children's needs are greater than your capacity to help them, go to your base's chaplain program and ask them to direct you to the people and youth programs designed to help you and your child through this challenging time.

De-Stressing On the Run

If you think you can't slow down enough to take the time away from work and activity to rest, then you need to read a book that Debi Stack wrote called *Martha to the Max* (Moody Press, 2000). She writes, "The key is to make breaks as different from work as possible. Vary the location, the body position, the activity level, the senses used—everything! Whether we're constantly on our feet or trapped behind a desk, there's something from the list below to help us to relax."

Here are a few of Debi's relaxing-on-the-run tips:

- Toss a Frisbee.
- Power nap.
- Listen to soothing music or praise tapes.
- Listen to an audiobook.
- Get a massage (I need to do more research on this tip!).
- People-watch on a bench.
- Sit in a library.
- Sit in a church and talk to God.
- Buy yourself a flower.
- Take a long lunch and see a matinee.
- Spritz your work area with a delightful fragrance.
- Arrange lunch with a friend at a park and swap the sack lunches you've packed.

Friendships

Thoreau said, "My friend shall ever be my friend and reflect a ray of God to me." Friends can cut our stress in half or multiply it by two—depending upon the kind of friend they are. Here are the different kinds of friendships I have found in our military career. As you'll see from the descriptions, some are worth having and others are not.

Regulation Friendships. These are the professional friendships we make with other spouses in the unit, the neighborhood, or at work.

While some may develop into lasting friendships, many of these are little more than acquaintances. Still, it's nice to have one of these special kinds of friends to attend a unit coffee with, take the kids to the park, or ask to help out with a school fund-raiser.

High-Maintenance Friendships. Life is too short for high- maintenance friendships. Let's face it, some people drain all the life from a party just by walking through the front door! We are usually drawn into these before we know what they're about. A good rule of thumb is: Listen to the way your new acquaintance talks about her other friends, because she'll soon be talking about you in the same way! If she's negative, complaining, and constantly giving you tips on who and what to avoid for gossipy reasons—then hightail it in the opposite direction as fast as you can!

Physical Conditioning Friendships. These are the people with whom you go running, attend aerobics class, power walk, play tennis, or swim laps. Some of these activities are more conducive to talking than others. For example, if you power walk, you have tons of talk time. With that in mind, be sure these are friends that don't drain you with negativity, ones that can listen as well as talk, and people who can keep confidences.

Temporary Duty Assignments. These are friends who come into your life for a week, a month, or a year—a very short time for a specific purpose and function. It may be that you will be the one encouraging them or vice versa. If we keep in mind that it's all right for some friends to be temporary, and the connection can still be real, then these people can be God's well-placed secret agents—helping us even as we help them in times of stress and need.

Deployment Friendships. It is amazing how a major deployment or war will bring people together. Sometimes I look at these as EMT friends, those who get us through an emergency-type situation. I've even been that kind of friend at times. We usually connect with these kinds of friends and bond deeply, only to have the connection fade after the conflict is over.

Permanent Duty Station. These friends are few and far between. We may have met these people during one of the above-mentioned activities or time periods, but these friendships stand the test of time, stress, distance, and bad hair days. When triumph is ours, these friends share the excitement—and don't get jealous. When tragedy happens—they are the first ones we call. Count yourself blessed if you find a couple of these friendships in a lifetime.

★　★　★

If I had my entire life to live over again, I don't think I'd have the strength.
　　　—FLIP WILSON

Name: Paquita Rawleigh

Birthplace: Jerez de la Frontera, Spain

Spouse's Name: Chief MSgt. Rodger Rawleigh, (Retired)

Kids: Three adult children, nine grandchildren

Branch of Service: U.S. Navy and U.S. Air Force

Years in Service: 27

Work: "Retired from Everything"

Hobbies: International Poet Society Award Winner, published in *Seasons of a Woman's Heart* and *Treasures of a Woman's Heart;* sewing; telling jokes and having a good time with her friends

Least Favorite Aspect of Military Life: when my husband went away, and I had to be alone with three kids

Favorite Aspect of Military Life: when he got back

CHAPTER NINE

Hidden Hero Portrait— Paquita Rawleigh

A Military Bride Charms America

*F*orty years ago Paquita Rawleigh was a new military bride who married a Navy third-class petty officer while he was stationed in her home country of Spain. They arrived in the States and had to in-process in New York City for a week. Fresh off the boat, the slender, pretty brunette got tired of sitting in her room looking at the four walls, so she decided to wait in the hotel lobby and watch the "foreign" Americans as they interacted. On the third day of her "lobby watch," she was approached by a man who spoke Spanish. She was excited to finally be able to speak to someone in her native tongue. They discussed a wide variety of topics, including American food, culture, and traditions. After several hours of visiting, the man leaned in closely and said, "Do you love your husband?"

She looked him in the eye and caught the full meaning of the inappropriate question he was really asking.

"Do I love my husband? Indeed!" she started yelling in Spanish, and then she showed that man just how much she loved her husband by hitting him over the head with her purse!

★ ★ ★

Paquita is an amazing example of the foreign military spouse, but she's also a role model for all military families in her ability to be spunky, tell a funny story, and stand up for what she believes. Most military brides that immigrate to the United States face a double whammy: they must learn the military lifestyle, *plus* they must also learn a new culture, complete with different customs and often a new language.

But Paquita says she "loves to tell stories and make people laugh." She coped with the difficulties of a new life by learning to look at the world through plastic glasses with a fake mustache and a funny nose. This upbeat outlook can be an incredible gift to those around you who are struggling—an amazing gift, in fact. Few do it as well as Paquita Rawleigh. This ability to create pools of laughter starts and ends with her brilliant ability to laugh at herself. She's had lots of fun recounting those days when her Spanish was far better than her English. Here are a few more stories from the "Queen of Fun."

When the Rawleighs attended their first military social function, she was embarrassed by the fact that she didn't know very much English, and her husband, Rodger Rawleigh, said that in order to learn the language she should "Mingle with people; just walk around and mingle."

She stood in the same place for several minutes wondering what in the world "mingle" meant. Then she looked around at the sea of faces and decided she needed to go to the ladies' room. As she was politely working her way to the other side of the crowded hall, she needed to get past a sailor, and said, "Kiss me!"

He stared at her, looking a bit baffled, to which she repeated herself firmly and politely, "Kiss me!"

So he did.

She was shocked, and reacted by slapping him across the face. Paquita's husband quickly came to her side and explained to the sailor, who was still rubbing his stinging cheek, "Uh, she doesn't know English very well, and she thought she was saying, 'Excuse me.' "

Recently Paquita decided she wanted to do something in her sixties to make her look younger. While her daughter has big bushy eyebrows, Paquita was not "blessed" in such a way. In fact, about thirty years ago someone told her that if she plucked out all her eyebrows, they would come back in fuller and thicker. So she did. But they never grew back—at all. So all these years she's had to pencil them in with an eyebrow pencil.

She says, "When I was junger, it was okay. I could see just fine. But now I no see so good. It is hard with my bifocals to see what I doing."

"Some days I look very surprised!" (Her eyebrows are upraised.)

"Other days, I look *very* angry!" (Narrow, furrowed brows.)

"And some days I just look confused!" (One eyebrow is up, the other down.)

So she went to an upscale beauty salon in her neighborhood to see what they would charge for permanent cosmetics that would give her a "happy" look. She entered the salon, went to the front desk, and boldly said, "Hell-o? Can chew make me loook ten jears junger?"

The receptionist looked baffled and went to get the cosmetic technician, who took an instant liking to Paquita and quoted her such a good price that this feisty woman replied, "Oooh, that eeese a verrry goood price! Tell me, is eeet for one eyebrow—or two?"

The tech laughed out loud and replied, "Well, for you, Paquita, it's 'buy one/get one free'!"

When Chief Rawleigh retired from the Air Force reserves, the Rawleighs moved from California back to their roots in Texas. They covered a lot of open territory as they caravanned down the road. Paquita was in her Mercedes 280SL sports car and got pulled over by the highway police on a lonely desert stretch in New Mexico. The officer stuck his head in the window of her car and asked, "Excuse me, ma'am, do you know how fast you were going?"

Paquita replied emphatically, "Jes, I go eightee-five."

The officer was solemn. "Yes, ma'am, and that's twenty miles over the speed limit."

The little woman was incensed. "No! It is NOT! I saw sign. It say eightee-five, and I no go more than eightee-five! I no should get no ticket because I go what the sign say."

The policeman's face flushed. "Ma'am, that's *highway* 85; the *speed limit* is still 65 miles per hour."

Paquita suddenly became quiet and replied, "Oh." She paused a moment. "It has been many jears since I drive deeze highways. I thought it fast, but maybe, I say to myself, maybe these people in New Mexico, they like to go eightee-five."

She peered at him under her surprised-looking eyebrows. "Are chew going to give me a ticket?"

The officer, whose mood had gone from solemn to trying to stifle his laughter, smiled and answered, "No, ma'am, I'm not; just slow down to 65. You're the best thing that has happened to me today!"

Whether she's telling stories to her girl friends or trying to escape her latest brush with the law, Paquita Rawleigh is a delight to everyone who meets her. Wouldn't you like that to be said of you? When she was being interviewed on the phone for the profile at the beginning of this chapter, she suddenly started to giggle and scream!

"Dere is a mockingbird who try to attack me every time I come onto my patio." (More shrieks and screams.) "She think I try to hurt her babies, and she chase me when I walk outside with de phone!" (Screaming and laughter as she hands the phone to her husband. You can hear her shrieking in the background as the killer bird attacks her hair.) Her husband patiently answers my questions about his time in the service, and then he hands the phone back to her. This time she's back inside the house. "I dun't know why that bird get so angry! I no want her babies, I already have my dinner today!"

Paquita has given the gift of laughter to her children, her grandchildren, and everyone who reads this book. The only thing she loves more than laughing is her husband. Her devotion to him, through all his military adventures and separations, has been one worthy of emulating. She's more than a hidden hero—she's my mom.

Celebrating
Community

CHAPTER TEN

A Time for Heroes
Military Speak Versus Spouse Speak

~

*I*t's not every day that you get to meet a legend—a real hero. Occasionally we get to meet other fighter pilots who have flown in World War II, Korea, or Viet Nam. We can sit for hours and listen to their war stories. Who would have thought that having one of these heroes into our home for dinner one evening would give me another "war story" to tell?

When Bethany was four, Philip was six, Daniel was eight, and Jonathan and Joshua were babies, we had the honor of hosting a celebrity author/ photographer in our home. Brian Shul was known in military circles for his books on the Thunderbirds and the SR-71. He's a true warrior, who was badly burned when his jet was shot down in Vietnam. In fact, he was told that he would never walk again. Well, not only did he learn to walk again but he also got back on flying status! Brian went on to become the A-10 West Coast Demo Pilot and then fly the SR-71, making the finals to the Thunderbirds in the process.

Eventually Brian began giving motivational speeches as a form of personal therapy after the war and his accident. In talking about his experience, he found healing and eventually became a much-in-demand public speaker. On a volunteer basis, Brian has shared his story with scores of Scout troops and other children's groups.

Bob had the privilege of being in on an aerial photo shoot as a featured AT-38 pilot for a book Brian was writing on fighter pilots. After the shoot, Bob invited this heroic man over for dinner. Brian has lived with facial scars for the past twenty years and is accustomed to children's natural reactions to his appearance. Nonetheless, we decided it would be a good idea to brief the children before he arrived.

We gathered our children in the living room. I took Bethany in my lap and told her, "Papa's friend has an owie on his face from being burned when his jet was shot down." Turning to the older boys, we continued, "He got burned while serving his country in Viet Nam; he's a real hero—one who put service before himself. So you don't need to stare at his scars or ask him a bunch of questions, because that would not be polite."

We were immediately besieged with questions like, "Who shot him down?" and "Can we look at him when we talk to him?" After we answered the children's questions, we felt well prepared for Brian's arrival—that is, until the doorbell rang and Bethany answered the door.

Bethany allowed Brian exactly two steps into the house before she announced in a characteristically loud voice, "I know why your face looks like that. It's because you got burned in an airplane." Brian, saint that he is, smiled at our three-year-old girl as Bob and I quickly tried to think of something to say to cover our embarrassment.

Unfortunately Philip was the one who came to our rescue. "Bethany!" he sternly chastised his sister in front of all of us, "Papa told you not to talk about the man's face in front of him!" Then our six-year-old turned to Bob and exclaimed, "Papa! Bethany's talking about the hero's face!"

Have you ever walked in the presence of greatness? Do you know how to recognize a genuine hero? Have you ever seen grace in action?

Well, in the middle of our profound embarrassment, we saw the character trait that made this man a genuine hero—grace. Brian smiled brightly and asked enthusiastically, "What's for dinner? I'm starved!"

We spent the rest of the evening listening to the life of a man who overcame many obstacles to serve God and country. For one night we sat at the feet of a legend.

★   ★   ★

Sometimes we take it for granted that we walk among greatness. In our community we have those who serve in quiet heroic ways, while others are called to make a more visible impact. Brian recognized Bob's commitment to duty to be equal to his own. Not every military member will be called upon to make such sacrifices, but the vast majority of them stand ready to do so. So be sure to hug your spouse and kids today—the heroes in your home.

When we were stationed with the Army, I met many families who were brand-new to the military, and many did not know how to tap into the community that surrounded them. Others were intimidated by the brave new world they'd stepped into. But the Army had a great volunteer program called "AFTB: Army Family Team Building" that taught both new and seasoned spouses about the military way of life. I took the course and then received training to become an instructor at our post. I so believed in the program that I was selected by the Army to go to Florida for a week of intensive master training. Once certified, I learned how to train the trainer. Much of the information in this chapter was acquired through this program, and I've selected the terms that are common to all four branches of the service. A list follows to better acquaint you with the terms, acronyms, and abbreviations that are common to the military lifestyle.

	Military Speak	Spouse Speak
Accompanied Tour	Tour of duty with family members	Lasts from a month (usually Hawaii) to ten years (in Minot, ND)
Active Duty	Military members actively serving and deployable	This means your address is written in pencil in address books.
Alert	Emergency call to be ready	What you're on when your spouse asks, "Are you in a good mood, honey?"
Allowance	Special pay and compensation	The amount you give your spouse from his/her paycheck
Article 15	Non-judicial disciplinary action	Their military career is over.
Benefits	Medical, dental, commissary, PX, etc.	Civilians see these as far better than they are for the military family.
Chain of Command	Leadership structure	Who you should be nice to whether you feel like it or not
Chaplain	Military minister, priest, rabbi, or pastor	Lifeline when life isn't in line
Colors	National and unit/organization flags	Found on a dress uniform shirt when Junior's crayons end up in the dryer
Commissary	Grocery store for military members and their families	Where baggers work for tips; payday the lines are longer than opening day for the latest *Star Wars* movie; and you usually can't find at least one thing you desperately need for dinner—like rice

Military Speak

Spouse Speak

	Military Speak	Spouse Speak
Deployment	A mission without family members	When the washer breaks down, the kids get a stomach virus, you lose your car keys, and your in-laws come to visit the grandbabies (and cook, clean, fix the garage door, and remodel your home, if you can get them to do it)
Detail	Job or assignment	What your spouse leaves out of the conversation, as in: "Uh, my TDY is actually to *Italy* but I guess I forgot to mention that part!"
Dining In	Formal social gathering for military members only	You'll always wonder what *really* goes on at one of these, since spouses aren't allowed to attend.
Dining Out	Formal social gathering for military and spouses	Don't *ever* throw a roll during one of these or it could end up in a formal food fight. (No, I promise I wasn't the one who threw it, and yes, it really ended in a fight!)
Discharge	Departure from active duty	Your life may finally become "normal"—whatever that is. (But you're probably going to miss the military just a wee bit.)
DITY Move	Do-it-yourself move	The goal is to get through one of these and remain married.

	Military Speak	Spouse Speak
Dog Tags	Identification tags worn by military members	Good for prying open cans of paint—but be careful you don't get the paint on the dog tag, because it's *very* hard to get it off!
Duty Assignment	Job/place while on active duty	We made it our motto to: "Never have a bad duty assignment." They are what you choose to make them.
Esprit de Corps	Morale within unit or organization	Another phrase for "I'm coming home late from work"
Family Support Center/ Army Community Services	A military organization that meets the needs of family members	You'd be a fool not to tap into this source of help—it's there for *you*.
Formation	Prescribed gathering of military members	A volcano-shaped structure that your eight-year-old makes with Dad's helmet in his sandbox, using water and mud
Frock	Assume the next higher grade without pay	More work. Same money
Gear	Equipment used by military members or civilian employees	Somehow you or the kids are held responsible when your spouse misplaces the little thingy part of the gear.
GI Bill	Education entitlement	Working four years for a free education
GI Party	Clean-up duty	What he gets to do when you cook dinner

	Military Speak	Spouse Speak
Guard	Members of the National Guard	What you stand on when leave is approved and you've already bought nonrefundable airline tickets to Disneyland
Hardship Tour or Remote	Unaccompanied tour of duty	When you're tempted to go home to Mama for the year or hire a full-time nanny
Hazardous Duty Pay	Extra pay for duty in hostile area	When you realize that even though they squeeze the toothpaste in the middle, put the toilet paper on backward, and work too many hours, you'd rather have them home safe than the additional pay for this duty
ID Card	Military-issued identification card	Make great cookie sheet scrapers, but you can't locate yours when you have to take your child to the emergency room in the middle of the night—and your spouse is TDY. (Hint: Look in the kitchen.)
Jungle Boots	Special boots for tropical climates	What you wear in your backyard when Dad is on a two-month summer trip. (Tip: Hire the neighbor boy to cut it.)
K-9	Special dogs trained for military police service	Call sign for anyone whose name starts with a K and has 9 letters in it, such as Col. George Kramlinger

Military Speak

Spouse Speak

	Military Speak	Spouse Speak
Klick	Slang for kilometer	The sound the garbage disposal makes just before you smell smoke
Latrine	Toilet	The name of the ugly witch in the movie *Robin Hood: Men in Tights*
Leave	Approved time away from duty	What gets canceled to improve morale
Orders	Spoken or written instructions to military member	These start arriving at the door when your spouse is gone and you've spent too much time watching the Home Shopping Network.
Power of Attorney	Legal permission for a person to act on behalf of another	A good way to get that new SUV the next time your spouse goes TDY to Hawaii (and all three kids have the chicken pox)
Protocol	Customs and courtesies	If you *forget* this at a military ball, it could *feel* like one of those scary childhood dreams where you're walking to school in your underwear.
Quarters	Government housing	What the *military* calls five kids in two rooms and *we* make it "home"
Rank	Official title of military member	The way your spouse smells after coming in from survival training
Regrets Only	Respond only if not attending	What will happen if you forget to go to the General's little party

	Military Speak	Spouse Speak
Reserve Component	Army and Air National Guard and U.S. Army Reserve	A regular life during the week and fun one weekend a month
Retreat	Bugle/flag ceremony at the end of the day	What your husband should do if he doesn't know the correct answer to: "How do you really think I look in this dress?" (And the correct answer is: an *IMMEDIATE* "You look great!")
Reveille	Bugle call/ceremony at the beginning of the day	A pipe cleaner used to make paper butterflies for the military member's homecoming
Roster	List of members	An excellent resource for finding people to invite to your Pampered Chef party
Short Tour	Unaccompanied tour, usually 12 months long	What it's called when it's *not* and you are left behind (There ain't nothing short about it!)
Space A	Space available	Never available in Florida in the summer, but usually wide open in Fort Drum in the winter
Taps	Last call of the day	The saddest song in the world
TDY	Temporary duty (off the installation)	Usually happens around birthdays, anniversaries, and holidays

Acronyms and Abbreviations

AAFES	Army and Air Force Exchange Service
AD	Active duty
AFN	Armed Forces Network
ASAP	As soon as possible
AWOL	Absent without leave
BAQ	Basic allowance for quarters
BAS	Basic allowance for subsistence
CDR	Commander
CDS	Child Development Services
CG	Commanding General
CINC	Commander in Chief
CO/OIC	Commanding Officer/Officer in Charge
COLA	Cost of living allowance
CONUS	Continental United States
CY	Calendar year
DECA	Defense Commissary Agency
DEERS	Defense Enrollment Eligibility Reporting System
DEROS	Date of estimated return from overseas
DOB	Date of birth
DOD	Department of Defense
DOR	Date of rank
EE	Emergency essential
ETS	Estimated time of separation
FOUO	For official use only
FY	Fiscal year
FYI	For your information
GED	General education diploma
GO	General Officer
HOR	Home of record
HQ	Headquarters
IG	Inspector General
JAG	Judge Advocate General
KIA	Killed in action
KISS	Keep it simple stupid/sweetie
KP	Kitchen patrol
LES	Leave and earning statement
LOD	Line of duty

MI	Military intelligence
MIA	Missing in action
MP/SF	Military police/security forces
MRE	Meals ready to eat
MWR	Morale, Welfare, and Recreation
NA	Not applicable
NATO	North Atlantic Treaty Organization
NCO	Noncommissioned officer
NLT	Not later than
O Club	Officer's Club
OCONUS	Outside continental United States
OIC	Officer-in-charge
OJT	On-the-job training
PAO/PA	Public Affairs Office
PCA	Permanent change of assignment
PCS	Permanent change of station
PDQ	Pretty darn quick
POA	Power of attorney
POC	Point of contact
POV	Privately owned vehicle
PT	Physical training
REG	Regulation
ROTC	Reserve Officer Training Corps
RSVP	Reply whether or not you can attend (repondez s'il vous plait)
SBP	Survivor benefit plan
SGLI	Servicemen's Group Life Insurance
SOP	Standard Operating Procedure
SSN	Social Security Number
TDY	Temporary duty
TLA	Temporary living allowance
USO	United Service Organization
VA	Department of Veterans Affairs

In concluding this chapter, keep in mind that when a family is new to the service, all these terms, acronyms, and customs can be overwhelming—kind of like taking a sip from a fire hose. Even military time is different: it starts counting at 1:00 A.M. with "0100" and continues until midnight (2400). If you're new, be patient with yourself and don't expect to learn it all overnight—Rome wasn't build in a day and neither is a military spouse. If you're not new, have an extra amount of patience with those who are new to the service. We're in this community together, and often the kindness of a veteran hidden hero to a novice inductee will make all the difference in his/her perspective.

CHAPTER ELEVEN

Operation Hospitality Check
I Volunteer to Have a Ball at the Ball

~

I was hosting my first coffee for the spouses of my husband's new unit. I wanted to keep the evening simple and decided to forego the traditional crystal, silver, and china. Since we were new to the area, I decided to center the coffee around a common military theme. So I decided to host a "moving coffee." The invitations were printed on packing paper glued to small pieces of moving boxes. We thought the entertainment could be assessing the damage of our household goods. (The latter is a joke, the former was not!)

Everything had to be nice, and several days were spent in preparing the food, house, and agenda. The table was decorated with boxes, packing paper, and claim forms. The cake arrived from the baker, depicting the Kays in front of our new house. There was a moving van in the background. The evening of the coffee, I put the finishing touches on the table, while Bob watched our youngest two, Jonathan and Joshua, aka Señor Mischief and his protégé.

Then their apprentice, Courtney, arrived. She was a two-year-old bit of feminine fluff who lived across the street. She was also the self-proclaimed president of the tricycle gang on Ft. Drum Circle. Her petite frame, blue eyes, and blond curls belied the fact that she could hold her own against my then three- and four-year-old boys.

Bob's temporary duty mission was to watch the little ones, which he did while he chatted with Courtney's father, our Army friend Trace, in our garage. They were discussing the finer points of artillery warfare when they were interrupted by a series of piercing screams. The shrieks, coming from inside the house, sounded like those of a woman who had just seen a mouse. The fact was, she hadn't see one mouse, but three. Their names were Joshua,

Jonathan, and Courtney, ages three, four, and two, respectively.

As Bob ran toward the house, the front door burst open, and he was run over by three blind mice scrambling out of the house. Their paws were covered with a gooey mess, their eyes shut tightly in fear. Behind them ran the farmer's wife, carrying a broom and shouting incoherently (thankfully, she left her carving knife on the kitchen counter). Inside, Bob saw the reason for his wife's wrath. While he was supposed to be watching the mice, they added another item to the Kays' list of damaged household goods: the cake.

★ ★ ★

Unit coffees are just one way military families celebrate community, such as the one I just wrote about. Another way military families celebrate community is through the customs and courtesies that give our families a sense of purpose, heritage, and pride. From the early camp followers to the diverse group of professionals and family members that we now have, our military is rich with tradition. These elements of community, for the military spouse, are always *voluntary*—you are not forced to participate in any of these conventions. As a matter of fact, most of the military awards for family members' volunteerism are tied up in the various aspects of military customs and courtesies, alongside other volunteer organizations.

These aspects of community can become a burden if we're not sure what they mean and how to participate in them. Not only does the military family need to balance its available time with volunteer commitments but it also needs to understand what the various customs and courtesies mean so it can rank order its priorities and participation in these events accordingly. For example, if a husband thinks his wife's getting an award and decoration at an awards ceremony is about the same thing as an office hail and farewell, he may miss a very important part of his wife's life. I've seen a few promotions where the service member pinned on a new rank and his wife didn't feel it was worth the effort to get a baby-sitter—so she missed a once-in-a-lifetime event because of a lack of understanding.

One of the most intimidating aspects of military life for a new spouse or a family who has recently joined the military is the "who, what, where, why, and how" of the various customs, courtesies, and traditions.

This section is designed to give you a better working knowledge of this part of military life. But it's more than mere definitions and terms. It is also chock-full of ideas as to how you can participate in a fun yet meaningful way in your own community—within your own comfort zone.

Here is a list of the most common traditions found in the military:*

A Note About Children

You should never assume that your children are invited to any of the functions listed below unless specified in the invitation or announcement. If they are allowed to attend certain ceremonies, such as your spouse's award, promotion, or change of command, they should be well behaved. (Our youngest, Joshua, still can't attend any of these functions—we've practically funded our baby-sitter's college education while we keep working on his behavior at public events.)

Reveille

The installation's American flag is raised daily, usually at 6:00 A.M., while the bugle call "reveille" is played. Everyone should stand quietly during this ceremony, unless you're still in bed, like most sane people.

Retreat

The retreat ceremony is held at the same time each evening, usually around 5:00 P.M., but the exact time varies from one installation to another. Unit formations, often including promotion or award ceremonies, may be held in conjunction with retreat. Then the flag is folded and retired for the day.

If you hear reveille or retreat being played, and you are in a moving vehicle, you must stop. (It is not mandatory for civilians to get out of their cars once they stop.) If you are outside, you should stand quietly, facing the direction of the flag.

Honors

Rendering honors means to stand quietly and respectfully. When required, a salute is given by military persons in uniform. If you are in civilian clothing, you should place your right hand over your heart. Honors are given to the nation, to certain individuals, or to the uniformed services; these are often represented by a flag or a song, such as the national anthem. When in doubt, follow the lead of the senior people present, unless you *are* the senior person present, in which case be aware that everyone will be watching *you*!

---

*Portions of this material have been adapted from AFTB handouts 1.01.

Parades

Official marches and reviews may include soldiers, vehicles, and a band and may be included as part of a change of command, an honors ceremony, a retreat ceremony, a retirement, or to observe a special holiday. Certain areas will be reserved for invited guests, and additional seating may not be available for everyone. These parades are official functions, and appropriate dress and behavior are expected (which means I have to leave my rhinestone-studded cat's eye sunglasses in the car).

Receiving Lines

At official functions ranging from a change of command to a unit social, you may be invited to greet the host, hostess, or guest of honor in a receiving line. Your name(s) will be given to the aide or adjutant at the beginning of the line. From there your name will be passed down the receiving line, but be sure to reintroduce yourself if there is a problem, without "correcting" the previous person in line. I've been in lines where it's like a game of "telephone gossip": I started out as Ellie Kay and ended up as Kelly May! Here are some more points to keep in mind:

- *Punctuality.* Arrive on time, because your unit will likely go through the line together. At larger events, guest arrival times are staggered so as to avoid congestion going through the receiving line.
- *Don't shake hands.* You will never shake the aide or adjutant's hand.
- *Keep it moving.* Receiving lines are for introductions only, not conversations.
- *No drinking!* Never eat, drink, or smoke in a receiving line. Often there are small tables provided by the line for leaving food, drinks, and purses.
- *Move along.* Do your part to keep the line moving.
- *Name, please?* When making introductions, be mindful of hyphenated names and spouses with different last names.
- *Ladies first.* Except for receiving lines at the White House, diplomatic corps, and **Air Force** functions, the lady precedes the gentleman in the line, even if the lady is the active duty member and the gentleman is a civilian spouse.

Teas

A tea is the most formal activity held during the day. It usually takes place between two and four in the afternoon. An appropriate church dress or suit is usually worn, unless the invitation specifies otherwise. It's considered an honor to be asked to pour tea, and a formal pouring schedule is often used.

Coffees

A coffee is a more informal or casual function and may be held any time during the day or evening. Dresses, slacks, skirts, and sweaters are acceptable attire, unless otherwise specified. I once went to a "sweatshirt and socks" coffee hosted by the commanding general's wife. Her desire was to be approachable and have a less formal function. We had to tell why we chose our particular sweatshirt, and the best "reason" won a prize. I couldn't decide which of two I wanted to wear, so I put my feet through the arms of a very large sweatshirt, and it looked like sweat bottoms when I pulled the hood up under my other sweatshirt—securing the hood with a belt. When I stood up to share, I told them I couldn't decide between the two, so I wore both. Then I released the hood of the sweatshirt around my legs, and it dangled between my knees like a tail. It was so funny that they gave me the grand prize!

Hail and Farewells

These are parties to welcome newcomers and to say good-bye to those who are leaving. They can range from office get-togethers to formal events. Spouses (and sometimes families) are invited.

Awards

The military presents many awards in recognition of service, achievement, or valor. The ceremony can range from an officer gathering to a unit formation. The award is read from the official orders, followed by the pinning on or presentation of the award. Spouses also may receive volunteer and service recognition awards.

Once we were at a meeting with one hundred other community leaders and spouses at the 10th Mountain Division in New York, where we were stationed. I forgot to remove my snow boots but figured they would be inconspicuous if I kept my feet under the table. I didn't want to go all the way out to the car to get my regular shoes. Suddenly the commanding general and his escort (complete with flags) arrived, called me up on stage, and presented me with an award with all the pomp and circumstance! It looked like a scene from *Ernest Joins the Army*!

Promotion

The military promotes individuals as they show an ability to perform at a higher level. At a promotion, the orders are read, and the new rank is pinned on. Family and friends are invited, and oftentimes the spouse will help the officiating officer pin on the rank. Promotion parties are at the discretion of the person who is promoted. Sometimes there is a reception on site or a party in a home, or the honoree buys a round of drinks for the O Club or NCO Club.

Change of Command

The change of command ceremony is a clear, legal, and symbolic passing of authority and responsibility from one commander to the next. The official orders are read while the unit guidon (or colors) is passed from the outgoing commander to the incoming commander. The senior noncommissioned officer also participates in the passing of the colors. Spouses of incoming and outgoing commanders are usually presented with flowers, and they should rise from their seat when accepting this honor. Both of the commanders represented usually make speeches, after which there is appropriate applause. At the conclusion of the ceremony, the new commander normally goes to the reception area, while the outgoing commander does not usually attend the reception. There is a receiving line at the reception for the commander and his spouse, and sometimes their children will stand in the line with them.

Retirement

This ceremony recognizes a person's years of service to his or her country and includes an official reading of the orders and presentations of certificates and awards. Attendance at a retirement ceremony is a thoughtful way to show appreciation for the person who is retiring. The spouse is usually presented with a certificate signed by the president of the United States. These are some of the most emotional events I've ever attended in the military, as one chapter ends and another begins.

Ideas for Community Coffees/Socials
General Comments

Coffees and socials, just like everything else in the military, are *voluntary* for spouses. The key to a healthy, vibrant, organized social group is to make these events a place where people want to be! It's got to be fun, brief, and serve a purpose. You can make it fun with the following ideas and a general attitude of thankfulness that your guests have made it a priority to attend (rather than the attitude that they are *expected* to be there and are only doing their duty). It can be kept brief by keeping announcements to two or three minutes each (if someone else is making announcements, be sure they understand there is a time limitation). Too often the business part of the coffee drags on forever because the person in charge feels they have to state the same thing five different ways.

Finally, a coffee needs to serve a purpose. Sometimes it has a dual function: fund-raising and social interaction; event planning and unit bonding; welcoming newcomers and volunteer recruiting. Be sure the attendees know the purpose of the coffee or social so that their expectations can be directed accordingly.

You never get a second chance to make a first impression, or so the saying goes. Remember that the very first coffee you or your unit host is likely to set the tone for the year, the tour of duty, or the group. As much as is possible on your part, put enough thought and preplanning into making sure that every person feels valued and welcomed and will want to come back next month.

Meeting People*

Life as a military family is too short to be shy about meeting new people. With a few tips and experiences under your belt, even the most reserved personality can learn to work a room with ease. Anne Abel, a retired General's wife, says: "Be genuinely interested in others. Everybody has a story and very few people will ask about you. Be yourself. At social functions my husband, Dick, will have met everyone in the room but I will know two to three people well." Here are a few of my favorite tips for first impressions, learning names, and how to meet people:

- *Eye Contact.* When you introduce yourself, remember to smile and make eye contact.
- *Handshakes.* Offer your hand, and give a nice, firm handshake, putting your thumb in the V of the other person's hand.
- *Remembering Names.* Repeat the name upon meeting the person and try to draw a verbal association with the name (i.e., "Nice to meet you, Steve Laube; I understand you're the editorial director for non-fiction at Bethany House Publishers").
- *Pronunciation.* If the person is wearing a name tag, visualize the name as you read it. Be sure you get the correct pronunciation. For exam-

---

*Some portions of this material have been adapted from AFTB course 2.011.

ple, the name "Laube" is pronounced "Lobby," but you might think it was "Lob," as many others do.

- *Party Pal.* If you're going to a party, ask someone to come with you who will know which people you will feel most comfortable with, and ask them to introduce you to these people.

- *Be Bold, Not Brash.* There's a difference between taking the initiative to introduce yourself and interrupting a conversation to do the same. If you wait for a break in the chatter, you'll find a natural opportunity to meet the others in the circle. You will likely be doing someone else in that circle a favor by helping them remember other people's names. It could be that they've had a fifteen-minute conversation without introducing themselves!

- *Be Confident.* One of the most common mistakes in conversing is to lack self-confidence and to act rejected by a perceived slight when there was none intended.

- *Body Language.* If you cross your arms, turn your back on someone, or keep your hands in your pockets, you are putting up a barrier. Whereas if you smile, keep your hands free to your sides, and look directly at the person talking with you, you will communicate positive body language.

- *Drilling.* Don't ask the other person a series of brief questions as if you were fact finding. It will appear as if you are invading their privacy. Keep the initial comments general and non-intrusive.

- *Monosyllabic Language.* Another common error in conversing is keeping your answer to one- or two-word responses, as if you have nothing to say or your thoughts are limited. The remedy is to try to answer in complete sentences; this will give you a chance to think of something else to say. For example, if the question is "Are you Colonel Kay's wife?" my answer would be, "Yes, I'm the wife of 'The World's Greatest Fighter Pilot.' "

- *Interaction.* An important element of a pleasant conversation is listening. Make it a habit to truly *listen* and to ask interactive questions based on the other person's responses.

Themed Coffees

Pick an idea, such as my "Moving Theme," and get creative! Below is a list of ideas to get you thinking. Remember to tie in as many elements to the theme as possible—everything from the invitation, to decorations, food, and even take-home souvenirs!

International Delight So many military families are world travelers that you could pick this theme and have everyone bring food and a souvenir from another county. During the icebreaker time, when you want to help people get to know each other, each person could show and tell a little about their souvenir. If you have a fun bunch of people, you could even ask them to come dressed in a costume from that country!

Give Yourself a Coffee This idea came from Anne Abel, who used to give a coffee for herself shortly after they moved to a new location. She invited all her neighbors in order to meet them. She also gave an annual "Love Tea" at Valentine's Day to show her friends and neighbors how much they are loved.

Tacky Coffee Rather than stress and fret about a formal coffee, try giving a tacky coffee instead. I did this at my house and pulled stuff out of my "garage sale" box to decorate with. I even put Elvis on Velvet for display by the front door. We gave prizes for the tackiest costumes and refreshments. The general's wife even got into it and came dressed as . . . me! (I didn't take it as an insult.) She wore a "Coupon Queen" sign (my alias) and carried a fistful of coupons. I must say, she never looked better, or should I say, "I" never looked better.

The snacks included Cheese Whiz on saltines, and one woman even brought a tray of vanilla wafers with cool whip and a peanut on each. You don't even have to dust your house for this one!

Restaurant Theme If you don't have time to host a monthly event at your home, check out a local restaurant that can handle the arrangements. Your group may meet for dinner at a different restaurant each time. You might even try to have it at lunchtime to accommodate those spouses that work outside the home. More and more coffees are being moved to central locations due to working spouses and busy schedules.

Wedding Theme Have everyone bring their wedding photos; number them and place them on a poster board. Have everyone guess who's who; the one who gets the most right receives a prize (such as a marriage book or a bouquet of flowers). It's easy to plan the menu around a wedding cake purchased from the local bakery, nuts, dinner mints, and other wedding reception goodies. The decorations could follow the same theme; you may even want to have a few of the bolder women share their favorite or funniest honeymoon memory.

Baby Shower I've been to some coffees that have a dual function, serving as a baby shower for the women in the unit who are expecting. Group gifts seem to work best for this type of event, but keep in mind that not every member of your unit will appreciate a function that serves as a baby shower. These are best reserved for the focus on the mom-to-be rather than a focus on unit business or announcements. That way if a member declines to attend, she won't miss any official news.

Ask the honoree if she wants games played on her big day and honor her request or decline. Be sure to have her fill out a very detailed list of items she needs or have her register at the local Wal-Mart or Target. That way there won't be duplicate gifts. Include this information on the invitation and indicate to whom checks should be mailed for group gifts.

You could have women send their baby pictures and have the same kind of game as was suggested for the wedding theme. Or, they could each bring their favorite stuffed animal or doll and tell the rest of the group why it's their fave.

Book Fest One way to keep to a theme and keep it simple is to have everyone bring their favorite book and/or the book they are currently reading. It gets people talking, and you get to know something about them that you would not normally know. Plus, it's a good way to get a tip on a great book that you may have overlooked in the past. (Not-So-Subtle-Hint: If you're reading this book, guess which one you could bring?)

Craft Fair Some people are incredibly gifted when it comes to creating something out of nothing. If you are one of these people, I envy you. A craft fair coffee is where the hostess provides the supplies and know-how to create a simple yet elegant craft that the attendees can take home. The hostess should have a completed version, and it should be simple enough for her to assemble in front of the guests. Have a couple of other crafty friends available to help the creatively impaired people finish their works of art. You could even have each guest bring her favorite homemade or purchased craft for show-and-tell.

Sweatshirt and Socks When we were welcomed to the 10th Mountain Division at Fort Drum, New York, the general's wife, Gloria Magruder, hosted this kind of a coffee, and it was so much fun (as previously mentioned). Everyone wore their fave sweatshirt and had to explain why they chose that particular shirt. We all took off our shoes at the door and remained casual and relaxed throughout the evening.

Mug and Muffin If your coffee is in the cold of winter or even on a Saturday morning, a mug and muffin coffee could be just the thing. Have each guest bring her favorite mug, and be sure to share why it is the fave. Have some unusual mugs to give as door prizes, and provide a variety of common and unusual muffins for the food table. Or, you could have the guests bring a half dozen of their favorite muffin along with the recipe (or the muffin mix box!). You might even want to have your guests bring along their slippers and have a large fire roaring in the fireplace to create a cozy and warm environment.

Pamper Night One of the best coffees I ever attended was held at a local upscale beauty salon. The staff let us have our meeting there and also provided catered munchies. Then they gave brief self-introductions with a list of their area of expertise and offered their services at no charge. They set a time limit so they wouldn't be there all night. We got free manicures, haircuts, facials, hand waxing, and eyebrow shaping! The salon picked up several good regular customers, and it was a win/win situation for everyone involved. They even brought in a licensed massage therapist and her chair to give mini massages. Ah ... I think I need to go back to her for more "research."

Ah, Crud! Let's Get Outta Here! Your coffee group could take a break from the norm and just have fun for one meeting by doing something different. Air Force fighter pilots play a silly game called Crud, which is a game played on a pool table, using two balls and your hands. It's so much fun the spouses have been known to have "crud parties" while the unit is deployed. Other groups get together for their meetings at the bowling alley or skating rink, and even the park—where the kids can play while parents take care of unit business. Some units have a game night or sundae-building party, where everyone brings a different topping. They build a huge creation and dive in. Be creative; have fun!

Keeping It Simple Army spouse Jody Dale says, "I'm not very good at coffees, but what works for me is simplify, simplify, simplify. Having just desserts makes the cooking time a breeze because you can start making these days in advance and put them in your freezer. I use outside branches, nuts, seeds, flowers, and weeds to decorate my table. If appropriate, I have icebreaker games, because it helps the walls come down and has people laughing and opening up."

Volunteering

There has been a national push under the direction of President George W. Bush to bring people back to the idea of giving back to their community through volunteering. The military depends on volunteers to keep programs running and to allow for a better quality of life for the community. Each year the installation volunteer coordinator presents a check to the installation commander with the equivalent of volunteer hours paid out at minimum wage. Last year our wing commander was presented with a check for the amount of $229,968.10 or the equivalent of 44,654 volunteer hours at minimum wage.

It's evident that the community greatly benefits from volunteers, but the volunteers benefit greatly as well. Here are five reasons for volunteering:

1. *Contribute to Community.* Your volunteer efforts often make the difference between allowing a program to continue and letting it fall to the wayside. That translates into areas such as your kids getting to compete in soccer games (volunteer coaches), young troops getting cookies at Christmas (annual cookie drive), families being able to buy household goods and clothing at reduced prices (thrift shops), and college scholarships (spouses' organizations). These are only a small sampling of programs that exist because of volunteers.

2. *Meet People.* Volunteering alongside others of like vision forges some of the best and most lasting friendships. Whether it's working with the Red Cross or helping out at the chapel—these are great opportunities to meet people.

3. *Support Children's Activities.* Our kids have outside interests that spark community service within them when they see us volunteering for their groups. Scouting programs, vacation Bible school, children's unit parties, and sporting teams are some of the ways to keep our kids involved and healthy emotionally, physically, and spiritually.

4. *On-the-Job Training/Enhance Résumé.* The volunteer hours you spend in certain areas come with training. Whether it's with the Red Cross in a hospital or on a computer at the Family Support Center, you are learning new and marketable skills while gaining valuable experience in a variety of fields. Your volunteer hours and awards on your résumé provide continuity for future employers as you move from place to place.

5. *Volunteer's Bill of Rights.* If you volunteer long enough, you'll find that as long as people are working in these different areas, there are likely to be some people problems. We don't live in a perfect world, and abuses do occur. I've seen a few people who volunteer at their children's expense, play the power game,

and run off anyone else who is a threat to their position. In order to keep the volunteer's perspective where it should be, AFTB (Army Family Team Building, Course 2.02.1 handout 4) has developed what I have found to be the best guideline for what you should seek out as a volunteer:

(1) The right to be treated as a co-worker—not as free help, but neither as a prima donna.

(2) The right to a suitable assignment with consideration for personal preference, temperament, life experience, education, and employment background.

(3) The right to know as much about the organization as possible: its policies, its people, and its programs.

(4) The right to training for the job—thoughtfully planned and effectively presented.

(5) The right to continuing education on the job—as a follow-up to initial training, to learn about new developments, and to train for greater responsibility.

(6) The right to sound guidance and direction from someone who is experienced, well-informed, patient, and thoughtful, and who has the time to invest in giving guidance.

(7) The right to a place for your work—an orderly, designated area that is conducive to working and worthy of the work to be done.

(8) The right to promotion and a variety of experiences—through advancement, transfer from one activity to another, and special assignments.

(9) The right to be heard, to have a part in planning, to feel free to make suggestions, and to have respect shown for an honest opinion.

(10) The right to recognition through promotion, awards, and day-to-day expressions of appreciation, and by being treated as a bona fide co-worker.

(11) The right to fun—a pleasant as well as a productive atmosphere for volunteering.

Recruiting Volunteers*

There are a few key steps to getting people to help your volunteer efforts, and most of them center on how specific and committed you are to your own goals! Here are a few things to keep in mind the next time your face is on the recruiting poster:

---

*Portions of this material have been adapted from AFTB course 2.02.1.

- *Be committed.* If you've lost faith in the project, you'll never get any-one else to value the assignment you're recruiting for.
- *Be descriptive.* Know exactly what you're asking the volunteer to do, how much time it will take to do it, and how this job fits into the organization as a whole.
- *Brainstorm.* This is a good way to explore sources of potential vol-unteers that could fit the requirement.
- *Matching.* Use a recruiting technique that will fit sources of potential volunteers. For example, if you're looking for public speakers for your group, approach toastmasters; if you're looking for soccer team assis-tant coaches, approach the youth center; if you are looking for baked goods for the airman cookie drive, send a note to the married families in your unit.
- *Benefits.* Be prepared with the knowledge of what benefits this vol-unteer job has to offer the volunteer and present them clearly.
- *Objections.* Listen carefully to the objections of involvement and do not proceed if it's not a good match. On the other hand, clarify any misconceptions that could be standing in a potential volunteer's way.
- *Materials.* If it is an ongoing job, have some printed materials avail-able for candidates to take with them.
- *Follow-up.* Be sure you check back with the person and also that you have their contact information. It is often in the follow-up that you are able to recruit the volunteer.

★   ★   ★

If you've been a military family for long, volunteering in your com-munity becomes a part of life. Your kids can earn college tuition schol-arships due to their volunteer efforts as you teach by practicing what you preach about community involvement. With time, attending social func-tions can be something you look forward to and participate in with ease and grace as you carefully pick and choose which events to attend and which to decline. You will find the balance that works best for you and your family.

Finally, the patriotic traditions of the customs and courtesies of this lasting piece of Americana can really get in your blood and be something you take everywhere with you. For example, last year I was at the world's largest honky-tonk, Billy Bob's in Fort Worth, Texas, for a post-event gathering of writers and publishers. Our little group was experiencing the Texas culture complete with mechanical bull riding (which I've done before), live bull riding, and a band called "Nighthawk." The group I was with thought I was a real jokester—and I was! At the end of their set, the band played "The Star-Spangled Banner," and my mood quickly changed to something more serious. I stood up and put my hand over my heart, while the people at my table just stared. A couple of them began to laugh, thinking that I was once again cutting up. But I looked at them and said, "Hey, fun is fun, but this is serious. This flag is why my husband flies and fights."

None of them were military, and they had never seen someone stand up inside a building when the national anthem was being played. One by one, each of them stood up and put their hand over their heart in respect for our flag.

★   ★   ★

Peace is that brief period of time when everyone stands around reloading.
—LLOYD CORY
Quote Unquote

★ PROFILE: ★

Name: Kathleen Harman

Spouse's Name: Com Sgt Maj Teddy E. Harman

Branch of Service: USA

Kids: Christina, Teddy, Mariah, and Matthew

Number of Moves: 17

Years of Service: 31

Work: accounting technician, Department of Finance and Accounting Service

Hobbies: quilting, cross-stitch, crochet, gardening

Volunteer Experience: Family Support Group treasurer, secretary, and leader; Family Readiness trainer; Army Family Team-Building instructor, master trainer, advisor; worked on rewrite of Level III Material in Washington, D.C.; American Red Cross volunteer, advisor; Army Family Action Plan facilitator, delegate; Enlisted/NCO Wives (Spouses) Club president, vice president, parliamentarian, secretary, treasurer; Girl Scouts, Brownie leader; Family Support Group co-leader/advisor for 1/15th Infantry, 3rd Infantry Division, Kitzengen, Germany, during Operation Desert Storm; 3/325 Airborne Combat Team, Vicenza, Italy, during Provide Comfort; 1/8th Infantry, Fort Carson, Colorado; 4/325 Airborne Infantry Regiment, 82nd Airborne Division, Fort Bragg, North Carolina; 1st Brigade, 10th Mountain Division, and headquarters, 10th Mountain Division.

Least Favorite Aspect of Military Life: leaving friends behind when we move

Favorite Aspect of Military Life: getting to know so many people of different cultures, traveling to different countries, and having the opportunity to make so many friends around the world

CHAPTER TWELVE

Hidden Hero Portrait— Kathleen Harman

Three Decades of Volunteering— (Does This Woman Ever Sleep?)

~

*K*athleen has been a military spouse for more than thirty-one years. She's lived through deployments, invasions, conflicts, and wars—not to mention the red tape she's had to hack through to get her four children enrolled in different schools for their seventeen moves in thirty-one years! She is one of the few active duty spouses who know what the Army was like, experientially, three decades ago! Consequently, because of this diverse experience, she considers one of her greatest joys to be able to help others become "all that they can be in the Army" lifestyle. In this section about community involvement and volunteerism, it's both enlightening and inspiring to look closely into the heart and mind of a lifelong volunteer—who isn't done yet! I've printed Kathleen's story in her own voice.

Why do you volunteer?

Kathleen: Here's my story: I met my husband after he returned from Viet Nam, and being a military brat, I wanted to settle down and live what I considered a "normal" life. We bought a small house, had a baby, and we were both working. Our life consisted of going to work, coming home, getting up the next day, and doing the same thing over again. After five years and three moves, Ted came home and said, "I just joined the Army—I leave tomorrow."

After the initial shock began to wear off, I quit my job at a check printing plant, we sold our house to make ends meet on an E-2 pay, and followed Ted into his new life. At the time, that is precisely how I felt:

HIS new life. Ted made E-3 out of basic, and we moved to Fort Polk, Louisiana, where he made E-4 and was promoted to drill corporal. He was really pumped up!

For our daughter, Christina, and I, it meant long days alone in a one-bedroom trailer. I had never driven a car, so we were isolated in the swamps of Louisiana. For three weeks Ted did not get off work in time to go to the grocery store. I finally got the courage to call him at work to see if he would be able to get off for a couple of hours on Saturday to take me to the commissary and get some groceries. Instead of getting Ted on the line, I got his first sergeant, who informed me that if the Army had wanted him to have a wife, they would have issued him one! Furthermore, he said if I couldn't take care of myself, maybe I should just go home. That went over *real* well.

I was beginning to think I did not like his NEW life very much. About a month later, the company had a cycle break and put together a picnic. The first sergeant came up to everyone as they showed up to greet us and let us know how happy he was to see us. I proceeded to tell him I was not an "issued wife," so he obviously did not have any concern for my daughter or myself.

Ted was quite embarrassed, and the first sergeant was at a loss for words. I could tell he knew I was referring to our phone conversation. The sergeant told me to remember that the mission comes first. I told him that if his wife needed food or his family had an emergency, he would probably rethink his statement. The only good that came out of that conversation was that a few years later he became a command sergeant major, and Ted and I ran into him. He still remembered me and would never forget what I had said. I hoped that somehow my words had a positive impact on the way he treated other military families. That was almost thirty years ago, and fortunately the Army has come to realize that part of the mission is preparing the family so that the soldier can do his or her mission without undue stress or distractions on the home front. Three months later my husband was stationed in Fort Lewis, Washington. We lived in a one-bedroom apartment, and again it seemed like he was gone all the time. A lot of the tenants were also soldiers' families. One of our neighbors had a little girl the same age as my daughter, and because we were both military spouses, we became fast friends. We had the common bond of being away from home and having husbands that shared a passion for the military. A couple months later it was Christmas, and we weren't going to have a Christmas tree, because with all the moves and Ted's E-4 pay, we couldn't afford to "do Christmas." On Christmas Eve, we heard a noise outside our apartment, and when we opened the door, there stood a small Christmas tree, decorated with lights and candy. Our neighbor and her soldier husband had tried to get back into their apartment before we opened the door—but I knew who had provided this Christmas joy! My two-year-old Christina was so excited! When I talked to my neighbor a couple days later, she said, "Through our soldiers, we have become sisters, part of a military family." She continued, "I know you would do the same for me, and that is what makes military families so special."

As Ted's career progressed, he wanted to develop the unit Esprit de Corps. I wanted to help Army families get adjusted to the new life and form networks and become what is known as the Army Family.

I believe these two very different experiences set the course for a challenging and exciting life as a military spouse. I also decided that I wanted everyone to feel like I did on that Christmas Eve rather than the isolation I felt with that first sergeant. I purposed at that moment to help others like the "sister" that lived next door helped me.

How did volunteering help you when your husband was gone?

Kathleen: Volunteering brought me in contact with people with whom I could talk because we shared the common bond of separation from our soldier husbands. Volunteering provided the opportunity to help someone else by sharing my experiences and information, which in turn helped me feel positive about myself. I found someone with whom I trusted my children, and we took turns baby-sitting for each other so we could go to the doctor's office, the commissary, a child's recital, or a baseball game. I found someone who was interested in quilting. I taught her how to crochet, and she taught me how to quilt. I also found a network of information and assistance when I needed it.

Did you volunteer during wartime or major conflicts, and how did that work out?

Kathleen: I volunteered in Family Support Groups throughout my spouse's career. During *Operation Provide Comfort*, we had weekly meetings to let families know any new information that we had about their loved ones. But most important, we provided the opportunity to talk and network in order to support each other. Through our telephone tree we were able to check on each other and let someone know if there was a need.

Sometimes volunteering makes the difference between life and death during a deployment. There was such an incident when we were stationed in Italy. The gas used in Italian heaters is odorless, so when the pilot goes out you don't smell the gas. A call was received from an apartment complex where several deployed soldiers' spouses lived. One of the spouses was feeling sick and wanted someone to come over and check on her because she did not know if she could get out of the building.

The key caller from the phone tree told her to get out of the building, and then the key caller called the rear detachment. They rushed over to the apartment complex. The spouse that had called was sitting on the bottom step outside the building. She said she was feeling a little better. The rear detachment then knocked on all the apartment doors and had everyone evacuate the building. When one of the spouses did not answer, they found the landlord and had him unlock the apartment. The pilot light had gone out on the heater in her apartment, and the young spouse (who was expecting a child) had succumbed to the gas while in the shower. It was an incredibly sad time. But we knew that we could have lost *several* more family members had it not been for the volunteers who were part of the phone tree.

How did volunteering enhance your résumé?

Kathleen: I didn't work outside the home when my children were small, but I volunteered at the school library and held several positions in the Family Support Group (now known as Family Readiness Group). I helped plan, organize, and decorate unit picnics, Easter egg hunts, fundraisers, socials, and unit balls/dining outs. When I decided to go to work, the only job experience I had was when I worked for the check printing company before Army life. When I filled out an application for government employment, I used my experience as the treasurer and Support Group leader for experience. I had outstanding letters of recommendation from the units as references. It jump-started my career with Civil Service as an accounting technician for the commissary.

The job I presently have is the result of that first SF171. I recently had ACS offer me a paid position teaching Operation Ready Classes to prepare units for deployment. This job offer was based on classes I voluntarily taught for clinics at the hospital. I turned that down because teaching deployment classes as a *volunteer* is a way of sharing with my Army family!

Have you developed friendships through volunteering?

Kathleen: I believe the best part of being an Army spouse for the last thirty-one years has been all the friends I have had the opportunity to make through our travels and through volunteering and networking with my "sisters." I often joke that I can travel across the United States, and instead of making hotel reservations, make phone calls and stay in the homes of friends. I have to admit that I need to change "sisters" to "Army spouses" because I have had the great opportunity to volunteer with a great spouse of a female first sergeant. He was the president of the Enlisted Spouses Club, co-leader of a Family Readiness Group during a six-month deployment, took care of his children, taught Army Family Team Building classes, and worked!

How has volunteering changed you?

Kathleen: I have learned that it is okay to be an introvert, because we are each unique, and it truly takes all kinds of personalities to make things happen. I've also learned, through AFTB classes on communication, that you have to receive a message as well as send it if you want to be understood. By taking AFTB classes and sharing that knowledge with others, I have learned to overcome my fear of speaking to a large group of people and have even been able to give classes on my job in front of my co-workers and leaders! I've gained the self-confidence to reveal my best qualities at a job interview, and I've learned not to sell myself short because of nervousness or fear! Through volunteering, I have learned that no gift is too small, and each of us can make a difference. Just giving thirty minutes of your day to help someone doesn't seem like much, but I know it can make a huge difference!

★　★　★

Kathleen is a wonderful example of how volunteering helps you as you help others. Not only did volunteering provide a healthy outlet while her husband was gone but it also gave her valuable experience for her current career.

★　★　★

The best volunteers are those who volunteer for something that interests them, something they care about. It isn't as important to possess all the skills as it is to have a sincere desire and the dedication to accomplish your volunteer mission.
—KATHLEEN HARMAN

Celebrating a
Balanced Budget

CHAPTER THIRTEEN

Budget Wars
Painless Budgeting (and Other Myths!)

~

I get more mileage out of a quarter than a Hyundai gets out of a gas can.
You see, I'm a born saver. I started saving money so early in life that by the
time I was twelve years old I'd saved enough money to fund a trip to Spain
to visit my cousins. I took three rolls of film with me and only took six
pictures, thereby "saving" two and one half rolls! Okay, I guess I used to be
a little compulsive about saving. I know how to save money so well that I
built a career around teaching others how to do things like feed a family of
seven for only $250 a month, pay down debt, and establish a workable fam-
ily budget.

On the other hand, my husband, Bob, is a born spender. When he was
a kid, his paper route money never even saw the inside of his pocket. This
pattern continued into his adult years, and when he became a fighter pilot
in the Air Force, he could still spend money faster than his Stealth F-117
could go from zero to 500 mph. For you Air Force novices, that's pretty fast!

So what happened when this spender landed in the life of a saver, and
she was swept off her feet? Well, I'll put it this way: Bob decided that he'd
rather dodge flying missiles in Baghdad than come home and tell me he
forgot to use the coupon on the pizza he brought home for dinner. Early in
our marriage, Bob unceremoniously deemed "budget" the "B" word. The
unmentionable sent him scrambling.

Now, don't get me wrong! Bob and I have a lot in common—we both
enjoy gourmet coffee and dark chocolate, and we like moving often with the
military. When we fly, both of us also like to rate the airline pilot's landing
on a scale of one to ten. Amazingly, we always rate the landings the same.
I've even been tempted to bring along markers and Post-it Notes so we can

each write our rating secretly and then hold them up to each other upon landing. It could be our own version of Mini Olympics for Pilots. As a matter of fact, we agreed on just about everything when we got married—except money. And yet we wanted to manage our finances as well as we rated a pilot's landing.

Bob and I are not the only couple with contrasting viewpoints when it comes to money—"finances" are mentioned as the number one topic couples argue about in marriage and are also cited for the most divorces. Money matters can be a real problem, even if two "savers" are married to each other, because they still have to decide on their financial goals and priorities. We found that an effective tool for working out our financial differences was that dreaded "B" word: budget.

Bob and I knew that if we didn't get a firm grip on our extreme approaches to money, we'd have to face some ugly consequences someday. Our "spending" consequences would include juggling bills and nasty calls from bill collectors, while an overemphasis on "saving" would only cause stress on our marriage. As the saver, I had to adjust my expectations for Bob—was it really reasonable for me to demand that he lunch at McDonald's only on Tuesdays, when they give free super-sizing? Was it reasonable for Bob not to expect me to get upset when he came home with a $200 power sander he bought on credit? Yes, we both needed to get a grip.

It wasn't easy for the spender in our relationship to get into the budget habit. We had some harrowing take-offs and hit turbulence while in flight. Initially, we went off and on our budget, straying one month and staying on target the next. I'd blow up when he came home with a used VCR that worked great and only cost $25—because he didn't check the Consumer Guide first! No, it certainly wasn't clear skies, but eventually with prayer and perseverance both of us found balance, and peace once again reigned in our home. That is, until we had five children in seven years; but that's another very long story.

★   ★   ★

Couples have cited "financial problems" as the number one issue in the majority of divorces. Therefore, getting a grip on your family budget could be one of the best "divorce busters" you implement for the sake of your marriage and family. Here are some financial statistics from a recent study* about debt and savings among members of our armed forces:

---

*Jim Fishback, *Defending the Military Marriage* (Family Life Publications, 2002).

- Thirty-nine percent of active duty personnel carry a balance from month to month on three or more credit cards.
- Twenty-four percent had personal unsecured debt payments of more than $600 or higher per month.
- Twenty-four percent have monthly payments that are one fourth or more of their monthly income (the national average is 15–20 percent.)
- Twenty-eight percent report that they had fallen behind in paying credit card accounts.
- Twenty-four percent have no savings, and 29 percent have savings of less than $1000.

Military families especially need to make their dollars stretch because of the hidden costs often associated with moves, TDYs, and deployments. Not to mention the meager pay of enlisted men and women in our armed forces.

Here's a sampling of nonreimbursable expenses to give you an idea how quickly things can add up:

Moves

- Childcare during a move
- Cost to have a military house cleaned for inspection
- Airfare and mileage to visit extended family members due to geographical separation
- Long-distance phone calls to stay in touch with family and friends
- More meals eaten out before and after the move and while unpacking
- Replacing lost and damaged household and personal items that may cost more than the allowable reimbursed amount. Or items that missed getting on the movers' log
- New blinds, curtains, rugs, carpet, drapes, due to the fact that those you may already have do not fit in your new home
- Increased insurance premiums on home or auto due to higher-cost area
- Increased rent beyond the COLA allowance

TDYs and Deployments

- Increased childcare costs
- More meals eaten away from home
- Airfare or mileage to visit family while spouse is absent

- Increased spending on entertainment as diversions
- A tendency to spend more on "guilt gifts" for the children
- Increased long-distance bills
- Impulse "pamper" purchases that rack up credit card debt
- Clothing purchases and "welcome home" gifts to surprise spouse upon return home

All of these costs are factored into a military family's budget, so there is a greater need to know where the money is going and to plan for the events that are a normal part of the lifestyle. There are services available within the military community, such as Army Family Services and the Family Support Center, that can also help your family develop a workable budget. With a little creativity and some hard work, you can aim high and fly with the best.

Hey, Where Did All the Dough Go?!

Begin your budget discussion when you are both relaxed. Breathe in, breathe out. Drink some warm milk. Have an Oreo. Have another one. Feeling relaxed now? No? Then try lighting an aromatherapy candle called "tranquility" and put on some Sinatra or James Taylor mood music. Better? Good. Now you can take your serene mood right into the budgeting process with you.

Now that you're relaxed, you can create your own budget worksheet by writing out the following categories:

Tithe—10 percent
Savings—10 percent
Clothing/Dry Cleaning—5 percent
Education/Miscellaneous— 5 percent
Food—10 percent
Housing/Utilities/Taxes—30 percent
Insurance—5 percent
Medical/Dental—4 percent
Recreation/Vacation/Gifts—6 percent
Transportation—15 percent.

The percentages and categories offered here are only guidelines.

Make three vertical columns beside the categories and title them: (1) Current Spending; (2) Spending Percentages Recommended; and (3) Actual Budget. Fill in the first column by figuring the average for each category for the last six months. Establish your total monthly income and fill out the second column based on the percentages given in the guideline. Leave the third column blank for now.

Bringing Home the Bacon

This is household income *after* state and federal income taxes and social security. Income includes salary, rents, interest, dividends, income tax refund, and other forms of income. Income does *not* include loose change found under sofa cushions. That would be considered a "windfall," unless your last name is Trump. Enter the total on the bottom line of your budget worksheet, under all of your expenses.

He Said/She Said

"I think we're doing all right!" he says. "I think we're doing pretty lousy!" she says. Now is a good time to decide where you *truly* are in your finances; it's hard to argue with the facts on paper. Take your net income and subtract your current spending to establish your overall spending pattern. Are you spending more (through credit) than you make? Did you realize you're buying $243.78 worth of pizza each month? Are there unexplained gaps in your current spending levels? Do you tithe? Did you realize that you frequented the ATM machine that much?

They're Singing Our Song

Families usually have favorite restaurants, movies, and even special songs that reflect the character and tastes of the family. Your budget will be just as unique as your family. It will be based on variable factors, such as your family's size, geographical location, debt load, and income. For example, housing can be a big variable due to your geographic location and whether or not you live in base housing. There are plenty of great resources to help you cut back painlessly on household expenses. As near as your base library, Barnes and Noble, or *www.amazon.com,* you'll find my books *Shop, Save, and Share* and *How to Save Money Every Day.* Be sure to check out the foreword, written by a certain reformed spender who just happens to fly jets.

Stay on the Same Sheet of Music

We realized that *both* of us wanted to try to have healthy finances, even though we approached money *differently.* As the two of you go through the sometimes painful process of establishing and sticking to a family budget, it is important to make a real commitment to these important issues.

We also realized that we didn't need to get carried away with the idea of putting our budget to work. We found that living on an austerity program strained our relationship, and we didn't want to become so detail conscious that the budget controlled our entire life. So we allowed an occasional indulgence, implemented budget-cutting techniques slowly, and modified the budget as needed. As time went on we fine-tuned some aspects of our budget and then had an annual check-up to keep it running smoothly.

Budget Busters

Since finances are so important in a military family, they probably deserve one more peek. There are a few problem areas that can throw a budget off course in a matter of seconds—sending it reeling toward disaster. Here are a few tips to avoid these pitfalls:

Debt, or Credit Some people have a policy of "cash only." Some couples set up an envelope system for cash. Every two weeks they place the budgeted amount of cash in envelopes marked "food," "entertainment," "gas," etc. When the money runs out, they stop spending until the end of the two-week period. A regular peek at the amount of cash left in each envelope is a vivid reminder of your budget commitment. If credit has become a habit, then you might even do something dramatic, like cut up your credit cards.

Impulse Buying Nothing busts a budget like impulse buying. If you don't have the cash to splurge by going to your favorite Italian restaurant, then don't go. If you buy compulsively at the mall, do your marriage a favor and stay out of that place! If you're an online buyer, spending money you don't have over the Internet, pull the plug.

Thirty-Day Rule A good way to short-circuit impulse buying is the thirty-day plan. If it's not in your budget, wait thirty days, thereby delaying the purchase. During that month, find two other items that are similar and compare prices. If it's still available at a good price and it fits the next month's budget, then buy it. You will likely find that you're buying less stuff because this delay gives you the opportunity to get beyond the impulse.

"Comfort" Spending Many couples find themselves indulging in comfort spending on clothes, sports equipment, expensive restaurants, and excessive entertainment, to name a few. But this is another budget buster you can't afford. Even cutting back on *some* of this kind of spending can

add up positively. For example, if you really can't afford to go out to eat four times a month, then go only twice.

Gifts Think about the gifts you buy for relatives, teachers, baby showers, weddings, birthdays, Valentine's Day, Mother's Day, Father's Day, kids' birthdays, and anniversaries. This doesn't even cover the biggie: Christmas. The first thing we should do is evaluate the "why" of gift-giving. Do we really have to give a material gift in each circumstance? Wouldn't a card work just as well in some cases? What about baked goods instead? Occasionally, giving a gift may even put the receiver under a sense of obligation. Think through each of these gifts to put them into perspective and save your budget at the same time.

Vacations A nice romantic getaway can seem like a dream and turn into a nightmare for your budget when you get the credit card statement. Some advance planning can keep this from becoming a budget buster. Consider all travel costs, including tickets for the theater or amusement park, tips, meals, and souvenirs. If you have to sink further into debt to accommodate your vacation, then simplify your plans until they fit your financial limits.

Every Mom Is a Working Mom

I've talked with scores of military spouses who work outside the home out of necessity, not choice. But how effective is this second income? How would you like to do all your work around the house, all the volunteer activities in church and school, and work outside your home as well?

Maybe some of you already have this lifestyle. Now, how would you like to do all of this with *no compensation whatsoever*? I'm not talking about volunteer work. We don't expect a financial return for that kind of work—that's why it's called *volunteering*. I'm talking about the other work you do—outside the home. It's ridiculous. Why would anyone work so hard for no compensation? Well, that's exactly what Sally was doing—and she didn't even know it.

Sally was an administrative assistant (or secretary) who felt she needed to work outside the home. Her family couldn't make ends meet without her financial contribution. Sally made an average wage of $7.50 per hour and felt she contributed greatly to the family's finances. She only had one child in day care, traveled a short distance to work, and paid no state income taxes. Then Sally attended one of my *Shop, Save, and Share* seminars and was challenged with the idea of "crunching the numbers."

She completed the form below and was shocked.

The amazing fact Sally discovered was that by working full time *she was making only $3 per week*! She didn't realize how those extra pizza suppers (because she was too tired to cook), and the trips to the beauty salon (to maintain a professional hairstyle), and all those lunches (away from home) added up! She realized she needed to make some dramatic adjustments. So she started taking her lunch to work and cut back on trips to the beauty shop. She found this didn't benefit her much. The sacrifices allowed her to make $30 a week. Wasn't her exertion and sacrifice (and fifty hours a week away from home) worth more than $30? She decided there was a better use of her energy and quit her job.

But Sally didn't stop there. She implemented some of the money savings ideas (contained in the next chapter) and is financially ahead of her professional peers. She has less stress in her life, and the freedom to contribute to her family's financial needs through saving money in the home. (After all, a penny saved is more than a penny earned). Sally discovered the incredible joy of sharing with those in need. She contributes her time and groceries to an eternal investment—people's lives. You see, not all compensation is measured in dollars and cents.

Sally's Salary

Gross Income per Week	Sally's	Yours
(40 hrs @ $7.50/hr)	$300	_____
Less:		
Tithe or donations (10%)	$36	_____
Federal Income Tax (15%)	$45	_____
Social Security Tax (6.65%)	$20	_____
Transportation (10 trips/8mi/.35/mile)	$28	_____
Childcare (1 child)	$80	_____
Meals/coffee (@$7/day)	$35	_____
Convenience foods at home	$25	_____
Extra clothing (includes cleaning)	$9	_____
Beauty shop	$14	_____
Other ("I owe it to me" items)	$5	_____
Total Expenses	$297	_____
Net Usable	$3	_____

Time Spent:

On the job	40 hours	_____
Lunch	5 hours	_____
Travel/Commute	5 hours	_____
Total hours away from home	50 hours	_____

Crunch the Numbers

You'll notice Sally is a bare-minimum example. When you crunch your own numbers, you may discover other factors, such as your family is in a higher tax bracket because your job puts your household income over the minimum allowed. You may commute farther than Sally, have more than one child in daycare, and eat more convenience foods. You may feel the pressure to have manicured nails, expensive suits, or any number of additional personal perks (because you work so hard and deserve those extras or because your job requires it). The important thing is to *honestly* assess your net usable income.

Once you come up with a figure, ask the big question. Is my time, energy, and effort worth _____ dollars per week? You'll be surprised at how painless it is to cut back and save your family a significant amount of money. It's not magic; it requires work and dedication. After all, not all compensation is measured in dollars and cents. You and your spouse may feel that having a rested, happy mom on the home front is worth some financial belt-tightening.

★　★　★

There's no reason for a military family to suffer financially because of a lack of resources. If there is an extenuating circumstance in your family's financial resources, you may qualify for programs offered by your branch of the service's aid programs. For example, the Army Emergency Relief fund regularly helps families with unexpected medical bills or those associated with hardship moves. The Air Force Aid Society helps families who have special financial needs as well. Plus, there are programs at your Family Support Center equivalent that will teach you and your spouse about everything from how to buy a car to investing and budgeting.

There's still a huge need for pay increases, and articulate, experienced voices like yours might be needed with your congressmen to speak out on behalf of the military family. But things have gotten a little better with the recent pay increase and a couple of other changes. Congress passed the Military Family Supplemental Subsistence Allowance (FSSA) Act about a year ago, which has effectively eliminated the need for military families to be dependent on food stamps. If you qualify for food stamps, you qualify for the FSSA, which is included in your pay. Once you receive the FSSA, you're no longer eligible for food stamps. WIC is another story, since it's a combination of factors, and while income is a primary factor, it isn't the only factor. That is another program to look into at your Family Support Center.

Financial sacrifices are another way that many military families contribute to our nation's freedoms. Most technical jobs in the military have a considerably higher pay counterpart in the civilian sector. And yet many of these families remain in the military. This indicates that financial compensation, while greatly appreciated, is not the primary reason military members serve their country. In this way, the family members, by accepting a lower standard of living, are contributing to a higher good—the freedom that our nation enjoys. So when you are tempted to grumble about the low pay and long hours or how the compensation is greater in the civilian sector, just remember that the work your spouse does is not measured in dollars and cents—it is measured in commitment to God and country.

CHAPTER FOURTEEN

A Penny Saved Is More Than a Penny Earned

Easy Ways to Save Money On Everything

W hen I married my husband, Bob, I got a "three-for-one" deal—which I thought was a wonderful bargain. Bob brought two precious daughters, Missy and Mandy, into our family, and they were a delightful addition! But our finances were not quite so charming. We had $40,000 in consumer debt and nothing to show for it. Bob was in the aerospace industry at the time and lived for the few days a month that he would fly in the California Air National Guard. He longed to get back into the Air Force and fly full time. That's exactly what he did six months after our marriage, and I supported his dream.

As mentioned in the previous chapter, the civilian sector often pays greater than the military, so we took a $15,000 a year pay cut to come back in. We ended up paying one-third of his income to Uncle Sam in various taxes, one-third toward the girls' child support, and 10 percent toward our tithe to our local church. This left us paying off that $40,000 debt while living on roughly 25 percent of Bob's income as a captain in the Air Force. We had five babies in the first seven years of marriage, plus Missy and Mandy, to make a total of seven children to support. And I wanted to stay home with my children, especially while they were young. If you do some quick mental math, you can easily understand why we didn't have money for groceries some weeks—even on an officer's wage. We supported a family our size on the financial equivalent of a Senior Airman. We needed a miracle.

And we got one.

Our financial miracle resulted in our family's becoming completely debt *free in two and one half years. What do you think happened?*

An inheritance?

The lottery?

A lucky trip to Vegas?

The answer to our financial woes may surprise you, but it is the premise of this entire chapter. The answer was found in something that is very, very small and seemingly insignificant: coupons.

★ ★ ★

Before I married Bob, I learned how to "coupon." I didn't have a financial need, it was just a fun hobby for me. After we married, I used coupons to feed our family. I got so good at slashing the prices for groceries that I started giving modest seminars to teach others. Then we started slashing our monthly expenses in other areas as well: clothing, household goods, and our vehicle insurance. All of these "little" things added up to big bucks. Let's do the math together:

If you can "save" $5,000 a year on the items we mentioned (we saved $8,000 on groceries alone last year—not including the other savings areas), it would be equivalent to earning about $6800 on the economy (by the time you pay taxes and social security). That is an additional $5,000 added to your family—free and clear! That is how a penny saved ends up being more than a penny earned.

We also did one other seemingly little thing that yielded big dividends—we prayed. We set up a budget, and we prayed for God's provision to help us stick to it and to get out of debt. Here's what's wrong with debt:

- Debt borrows on your future.
- Debt makes you a servant to the lender.
- Debt places financial stress on your marriage and family.
- Debt erodes resources through high-interest payments.
- Debt promotes impulse buying.
- Debt limits your ability to be generous.

But how do you get $40,000 out of debt and live on so little at the same time? One thing we did after we decided to get on a budget and get out of debt was to apply every bonus, unexpected check, or financial gift toward our debt. Here were just a few of the checks that came our way:

- USAA insurance premium refund
- GI Bill for Bob's master's program reimbursement (six years after he finished the program)
- Christmas checks from relatives
- *The Price Is Right* (I went on the show and won a prize that we sold for cash)
- Military bonus for signing a five-year commitment

All of these miracles, we believe, happened because we were finally committed to being good stewards of our financial resources and to tithing a percentage to our local church. But while these checks helped pay down our debt, they didn't pay the living expenses we had. That happened because we learned to stretch the value of a dollar. The old saying "Necessity is the mother of invention" was never more true than in the Kay household in those early years.

But the story doesn't stop there. I developed an uncanny ability to save on practically everything a family must buy. My seminars were mainly given to teach other families how to do the same thing, and I did it on a volunteer basis as my way of giving back to the community.

By the time we reached Holloman Air Force Base in 1997, my seminars came to the attention of Lenn Furrow, the director of the Family Support Center. She saw that the quality of life of hundreds of HAFB families was being positively impacted by my *Shop, Save, and Share* seminar, and she approached the Air Force Aid Society to fund a film project. They made this seminar into a video that was distributed to 120 Air Force bases around the world, and it began to make an international impact on military families.

But once again, the story doesn't stop there. The seminar came to the attention of a senior editor at Bethany House Publishers via an author friend, Becky Freeman. This editor, Steve Laube, was impressed with the distribution of the seminar and saw a potential to reach many more families with a book. So Bethany House published *Shop, Save, and Share* in 1998. Steve later told me that there was a 1 percent chance that my book would get published (the percentage of unsolicited manuscripts that get published).

In addition, Crossings Book Club picked up the book, and it sold so many copies that it made their bestseller list. The success of the first book led to *How to Save Money Every Day,* published in 2001, and *Money Doesn't Grow On Trees,* published in 2002. I currently have four more books under contract. God has exceeded all my dreams and expectations of getting the *Shop, Save, and Share* message out to those who can be helped by it. I've become a guest commentator on a national radio program, a regular guest on CNBC's #1 rated *Power Lunch,* and have had the profound privilege of helping raise millions of dollars to feed hungry children in developing countries via *Life Today's* annual nationally televised hunger campaign.

So why did this miracle happen to our family? Well, the answer can be found along the lines of The Little House That Jack Built:

1. We were committed to getting rid of $40,000 in debt.

2. Lenn Furrow had a desire to help Air Force families with my program.

3. Bestselling author and friend Becky Freeman had a vision not only for helping me but also for helping others through the message and methods God gave me, and gave the book to the right editor.

4. This editor, Steve Laube, caught the vision and saw to it that through this book thousands of families in need of real-life tools to get them on solid financial ground would get the message.

But did it all really start with a commitment to get out of debt?

No.

It started because we had a huge financial problem.

Sometimes a destiny is an opportunity wrapped up in a problem.

★   ★   ★

Whatever your challenges are, you can do more than live through them—you can rise above them! Furthermore, if you persevere beyond the problems of today, you will be in a position to be a source of hope to others.

Our financial problems became the opportunity to fulfill my destiny of helping others manage their money better. If you find yourself in similar circumstances, my books offer a detailed, realistic approach to putting debt behind you and your destiny before you. Even if you are not currently experiencing financial difficulties, you still may want to save a substantial amount each year in painless ways! Whether you *want* to save or you *have* to save, here are the best tips I've gleaned from my experience. While they are not exhaustive, they will get you started.

Insurance

I was an insurance broker for several years before I met and married Bob. This is one area where a few minor changes could yield big savings.

There's a chart on the next page to help you navigate your way around life insurance policies. Also, be sure you have the maximum coverage offered by SGLI, Serviceman's Group Life Insurance. It is purchased through the military, and you won't find a less expensive source for insurance as a military service member. In addition, here are some quick ways to reduce insurance premiums for your automobile and household goods:

USAA This is a great insurance company for military families. Not only do they cover auto and homeowner's insurance but they also offer dividends back on policies at the end of the accounting year. The longer you are with the company, the greater your dividend check. We've received anywhere from one hundred to almost one thousand dollars, which is an unexpected source of income. Plus, they pay their claims quickly and efficiently. Bob has been with them for twenty-five years!

Homeowners Carry only the coverage you need. If your home is valued at $100,000, and you insure it for $120,000, and it burns down, they will only pay $100,000, and you've overpaid the premium. Keep in mind also that the insurance price of the home does not include the land.

HOB The Homeowner's Broad form at 90 percent of the value of your home is what you want to cover with replacement value. That way, if your hot water heater breaks and floods your carpet, you'll be reimbursed for what it costs to replace the carpet rather than a devalued price on the carpet that won't come close to replacing it.

Homeowner's Deductibles Carry a $500, $1000, or 1 percent deductible on your homeowner's policy.

Special Riders Check with your insurance company to see their limitations on personal articles. Jewelry, collections, antiques, computers, and guns may all need to be added as riders to get the full coverage on these personal items. Insurance companies will only cover a minimum on these without a rider.

Flood Insurance Remember that flood insurance is only sold by the state, and you are not covered unless you've purchased this policy from the government.

Tenant Policies If you do not own your home or you live in military housing, you will need to get a tenant policy. Ask for a nonsmoker's discount if you qualify, and shop around. You will want to get replacement value and special riders if necessary.

Automobile—Mutual Risk Drivers If you or your spouse has a less-than-perfect driving record, you are considered a greater risk to insure. The same applies to young drivers under twenty-five years of age. Put these drivers as the principal driver on a vehicle that does not carry full coverage. You might have to put a car title in a teenage driver's name in order to be able to do this. Check with your agent, because the rules on this vary from state to state. Taking driver's education is another good way to get a ticket off your record or a discount on your policy.

Uninsured Motorists If you are driving a car that does not carry full coverage (comprehensive and collision), the state requires that it carry at least liability coverage. Part of the basic auto coverage package is medical and uninsured motorists. These two portions of a liability package can be excluded with your signature on a form in some states. However, it is not advisable, because the savings are minimal. And more important, in the event of an accident in which the other person is at fault and they don't have insurance, your auto and medical expenses will be covered.

Discount City There are often tons of discounts on your homeowner's policy, and especially your automobile policy, that are yours for the asking. For homeowners, you can get discounts for a security system, tile roof, fenced yard, nonsmoking household, gated community, or enclosed garage. For automobile policies, ask for discounts for driver's ed, safe driving records, security systems on a car, an enclosed garage, non-smoker's policy, drivers aged thirty to sixty, multi-car discounts, and military discounts. Purchasing auto and homeowner's insurance within the same company will also sometimes qualify you for special discounts.

Bonus Tip Young Drivers—If you have a teenage driver, ask your insurance agent to give him/her an informative talk about driving safely and responsibly. Ask the agent to give your child examples of how much insurance can cost if they get one ticket or have an accident. We did this when I was an insurance broker, and it seemed that kids received counsel from a professional better than they would from their parents.

Everything You Wanted to Know About Life Insurance
(But Were Afraid to Ask)

Type of Insurance	Advantages	Disadvantages
Level term	Level payments over specific period, usually 5, 10, 15, or 20 years; may be convertible to a permanent policy	More expensive than ART in early years; less expensive in later years.
Whole life (permanent)	Fixed premiums; cash value you can borrow against; possible dividends; tax-deferred earnings; guaranteed death benefit.	Initially higher premium than term insurance; little flexibility in premium payments
Universal life (permanent)	Flexible premiums; tax-deferred earnings on cash value; access funds; different options allow cash buildup or insurance protection.	If interest rates fall, low cash value buildup may cause policy to lapse unless you add money.
Variable life (permanent)	Fixed, level premiums; guaranteed death benefit; choice of investment options.	You assume risk for policy's cash value; rate of return varies with investments chosen.
Annual renewable term (ART)	Most coverage for the least money; protection in increments of one year; can renew yearly up to specified age (usually 70); may be convertible to permanent policy.	Premiums start low but rise with each new term; nothing back if you outlive contract.
Variable universal life (permanent)	Similar to variable life but with flexible payments. You select the investment vehicle that generates your cash value growth (stocks, bonds, etc.).	Potentially higher earnings than other cash value policies, but also greater risk.

Buying a Car

The least expensive car for you to drive is probably the paid-for, older vehicle you are now driving! People talk themselves into a car for a variety of reasons. Take, for example, gas mileage. When you actually calculate gas mileage and the money you "save" when compared to interest payments and depreciation on that new car, you will find that you do not even come close to saving money. The average new car depreciates roughly 30 percent within the first eighteen months, with an average loss of value of five thousand dollars as soon as you drive it out of the parking lot. So look for a used vehicle before you consider new.

However, when interest rates are incredibly low or a family needs the warranty (because of high mileage), it may be best to get a new car. Try to get an end-of-the-year clearance model, a demonstrator model, and, if possible, buy it in December or January—which are the leanest months in the industry. The following tips can apply to buying a car new or used.

Negotiate these three sales points separately:

Price Negotiate the price of the car at a dealership apart from the value of the trade-in. Tell the salesperson you want to determine the price of the car without a trade-in. The reason you want to do this is because salespeople will often give you far more for your trade than you expected—thus hooking you on the deal. However, they discount the price accordingly—giving you less of a discount because of the additional amount they've put into your trade. Look up the value of the car at *www.edmunds.com,* print out the page, and bring it with you to the car lot.

Trade-ins Now that you've determined the price of the car, ask what the dealer will give you for your trade-in. Most *honest* dealerships will tell you that you will get more for your car if you sell it yourself. A little elbow grease and some top-notch detailing can net you hundreds of dollars more than a dealer can give you. But military families don't always have the time to do this due to moves, TDY schedules, and courses. Again, to determine the value, go to *www.edmunds.com.* Not only does Edmunds' car-buying guide list new car prices, used car prices, car comparisons, and car-buying advice but they also give car ratings, car values, and auto leasing prices. Remember to print out the page listing your car and bring it to the dealership with you. You could also try the Kelley Blue Book site at *www.kbb.com.*

Financing The finance and insurance office is where the lion's share of a dealership's profit is made. In this office, you will have to navigate interest rates, payments, terms, and warranties. Unless you put miles on your car for business, the extended warranties are usually not a good value. Also, you can generally do better on interest by selecting your own creditor, and the credit life insurance they offer is more expensive than raising your regular insurance premium by $20,000 to cover this expense.

Food and Household Products

The first third of my book *Shop, Save, and Share* is devoted to this topic, as well as a couple of chapters in *How to Save Money Every Day*. I currently feed our five school-aged children (including a 6'4" fifteen-year-old son) for $250 a month. This includes toiletries, household cleaners, and medicines. It may sound amazing, but if you go to the book review page of *Shop, Save, and Share* at *www.amazon.com,* you'll find scores of people across the country who are now doing the same. Here are the main points to remember:

Buy Low Try to make it a point never to buy anything full price, unless its regular price combined with a coupon makes it a good value.

Sale Ads Get your local paper to have the sale ads delivered to your door each week. To find out the sales at the commissary, go to *www.commisaries.com.*

Match Values Make out your shopping list by what is on sale. Combine coupon values with the sales to determine if the item is worth buying.

Coupons In *Shop, Save, and Share,* I spend an entire chapter discussing the differences between the eight kinds of coupons available to consumers. By knowing your coupons, you also know which ones can be combined for greater savings. For example: a manufacturer's coupon (reimbursed by the manufacturer) can usually be used in conjunction with a store coupon (reimbursed by the store—such as Walgreen's. If they're marked "military coupons," they are still manufacturer's coupons, not store coupons). There are photos as well as definitions in that chapter to help distinguish between the various types of coupons.

Locating Coupons Many family support centers have swap boxes. Check yours, and if it doesn't have one, consider starting one yourself. Go to *www.elliekay.com* for links to free coupons, and never pay for a manufacturer's coupon. The best resources are the FSIs (Free Standing Inserts) in your Sunday paper. Look on products, on pull boards attached to the aisle, and even electronic coupon dispensers in the store.

Greek to Me The coupon definitions may seem like Greek to you right now, but after you've read up on it in SS&S and practiced it a few times, it will translate into hundreds of dollars of savings annually—or, for thousands of readers, it could mean even thousands of dollars!

Shop With a List Someone who shops with a list and sticks to it (except for sales and other discounts) will save close to 30 percent more over someone who doesn't.

Time Savers People often tell me, "I don't have time to use coupons; I have a life!" Well, if you're organized, it only takes about two hours to use coupons effectively. To save time, use an aisle order chart (get these at the customer service desk; they are a map of the store) and make out your list according to aisle order.

Pull out as many coupons as you can at home, and put them in a coupon envelope (a legal-sized envelope marked with the name of the store). Also, if you will buy three to four copies of the Sunday paper and match up the like facings of FSIs, you can make one cut to cut out four copies of the coupon at the same time.

Share Once you've followed this system for a while, you'll find that you're getting tons of stuff free or for only pennies. Consider sharing groceries with the local homeless shelter, crisis women's center, or the Salvation Army—or even the family up the street who has a need.

Garage Sales

These are a way of life for military families—it seems you're either having one or your neighbor is. But these can also be a great source of saving money if you do it the right way. Here are the top ten tips to garage sale success:

1. *Leave Them Home.* We love our kids, but if at all possible, leave them at home, and you'll do better at a garage sale. You'll leave at o'dark hundred, and you'll need to concentrate.

2. *Bargain.* Don't pay more than you are comfortable with for a given item, but balance that with the fact that people have gone to a lot of work to make some extra money. I think the best rule of thumb is to say, "What am I willing to pay for this?" Then ask the seller if he'll take the lower amount you're willing to offer. If the price is reasonable, eight times out of ten they'll take your lower price offer.

3. *Strategize.* You'll need to develop a plan of action. First of all, think about the things you're looking for in a garage sale and make a list. Categorize your clothing, making a complete inventory. Determine the right

sizes of the people in your family. If you buy things too small, you'll be wasting money. Do you need a new bike for Johnny? Could you really use a good snowblower? Determine the items you need to buy within the next two to three months and put them on your list.

4. *Plan.* Get a newspaper with the garage sales listed in it and get a good city map. Note the opening times and the items advertised in the notices. Prioritize the garage sales according to the advertised items you need most, and then plan your route accordingly. You may want to start in the area with the earliest openings. Visit all the sales in the same area to save time and money. Don't arrive sooner than the set opening time—sellers won't have all their things set up yet, and they won't be in a negotiating mood that early in the day either. The sales you visit later in the day are more likely to yield a bargain, as anxious sellers will ask you to "make an offer."

5. *Friends.* If you go with a friend, agree on the same strategy. If you can't agree, then go alone. Brenda Taylor was one of my all-time best garage sale buddies—she and I think alike! I really miss Brenda. Sometimes this military life stinks; that is, when it takes you away from your friends. Ah, but I digress.

You probably won't have the time (or energy) to hit all the sales, so keep your trips to each house short and sweet. It might be a good idea to take along some coffee and snacks if you're going to be out for several hours.

6. *You Aren't Saving Anything If You Don't Need It!* Unlike grocery shopping, I don't buy things at yard sales unless there's a specific use for them. It isn't saving if you're just shopping. A good garage sale mindset is: buy goods you will have to buy anyway. For example, if you find a pair of pantyhose still in the package, in your size, for a quarter—buy them! You would pay at least $3.00 for them elsewhere, and you've just saved $2.75! If you'll never wear them, however, because they're two sizes too small, you've just wasted 25 cents.

7. *If It's Broken, Don't Buy It!* People have garage sales for different reasons. Everything on their tables and hanging in their awnings is there for a reason. Sometimes the reason is that it's broken. So if you can't plug it in, put a battery in it, or start it—then don't buy it, because it's probably broken. Life is too short to buy things you need to repair—unless you know what you're doing.

8. *If It's Stained, Leave It.* You can afford to be choosy at a garage sale. If it's dirty and can easily be washed, buy it. But if it's stained, or you

can't tell, leave it on the table. There are quality products for sale at garage sales that are in great shape. You don't have to settle for second-rate goods. Look for clothing with sales tags still on them and products in their original packaging.

Check the zippers, buttons, and snaps on clothing. Pick and probe gadgets to make sure they work well. Count the accessories to a game to make sure all the pieces are there. Look pottery over carefully for nicks and dings. Check the knees on jeans to determine wear and tear. Look at the size on a curtain opening to make sure you have the right size curtain rod. It's not a bargain to buy $5 curtains when you have to pay $25 for a custom curtain rod in order to hang them!

9. *Can This Marriage Be Saved?* People get rid of new things for all kinds of reasons. I love the *newlywed sales*. They have wedding gifts (they didn't like or cannot yet appreciate) still in boxes. Or, they have duplicate toasters, microwaves, and coffeemakers. My garage sale buddy, Brenda, bought a new coffee grinder for $2 at one of these sales. Regularly, we pick up brand-new silver, crystal, and china at newlywed sales and keep them on hand for hospitality gifts, wedding gifts, or even a birthday gift here and there. There's absolutely no difference between paying $45 for a silver chafing dish at Service Merchandise and paying $8 for the same piece, still in the box, at a yard sale.

10. *Estate Sales.* These sales have many of the same bargains, especially on antiques. Check the appliances carefully at these sales, though, as they tend to be well-worn, older units. But if you know what you're looking for, you can find a diamond among the coal.

If you live near a university that has family housing, you can find some great deals at yard sales. At the end of each semester, especially in May, families sell off household goods they can't take with them. It's worth a peek!

Hit the *wealthy neighborhoods.* Most of these people have never been to a yard sale and don't know how to price many items. If anything, they tend to price their items lower than other yard sales because they don't know common prices—or they don't care. If an item is overpriced in these sales, you can make a comment about its price: "I usually find shoes like these for $2 at most garage sales." They will often give it to you for the lesser amount. It's a great way to get name brands. I've even found a few Neiman Marcus labels at these sales!

Two Kinds of Garage Sales

I've taken our oldest son, Daniel, to a lot of garage sales with me lately—it's not like taking the whole herd. Daniel understands the ground rules of advance garage-saling. He's learning the fine art of bargain hunting too. He knows not to bother me when I'm concentrating on the search or bargaining with the seller. He spends his own money, and he spends it judiciously. He does his own bartering and is rarely turned down when he asks for a lower price. Daniel has already learned there are basically two kinds of garage sales.

The first kind is where *they want to get rid of stuff* and the second is where *they want to make money.* In the military we see a lot of the first kind of garage sale—they're our favorite. They have things priced to sell or even give away. Military families move a lot and only have a certain weight allowance. They have to trim the extra fat and get rid of the things they can't take with them.

As I said, the second kind of garage sale is where they want to make money. Daniel and I don't like these garage sales as much, and we don't stay long. Most of the stuff at these sales is overpriced (for a garage sale), and the folks get defensive if you ask them to take less. There are too many good sales out there to waste time on an overpriced garage sale. The irony of these two sales is that the first kind makes more money than the second because of the volume they sell.

Stay on Budget

Garage sales need to be a part of your monthly budget. We usually budget $50 a week. This covers even the major garage sale purchases in the long run. The garage sale benefit greatly diminishes if you go over budget to save money. It defeats the purpose of shopping these sales. If you're one who is given to impulse buying, leave your checkbook and wallet carefully hidden in the car. While you're walking back to your vehicle to get your money, you'll have time to think about your purchase and decide whether you really need it or not.

Cheap Thrills! Garage-saling is fun! I go out for two or three hours and come back with $300 worth of merchandise for which I paid $30. Let's see, that's a savings of $270 divided by three hours for a total of $90 per hour. There's a psychological boost involved in the savings game and in seeing how we can save in the little ways; plus, you also get to relieve yourself of the urge to shop!

Bonus Tip: How to Have a Successful Garage Sale

If you're thinking of having a garage sale, then look over this list before you commit. It does require a lot of work and time for the profit you will make. Some families may decide that donating their items to the Salvation Army for a $500 tax-deductible receipt is a better option for them than the effort of a garage sale.

However, if you decide that you have enough time and energy, follow these steps to garage sale success!

Collect Throughout the year, throw stuff in a big box marked "Garage Sale." You'll be amazed at how much you collect. This also helps relieve clutter—thereby relieving stress. Once you see how much junk you have, you'll know whether you have enough for a garage sale or whether you need to buddy up your sale with a neighbor or friend.

Locate Choose your location carefully. The ideal place to have a garage sale is in a neighborhood where these sales are common. If you live in an out-of-the-way or hard-to-find location, you probably won't have a successful sale.

Advertise If you live in an area where garage sales are common, you won't need to advertise—a good sign will suffice. Otherwise, take out a small ad in the local newspaper or the *Thrifty Nickel*. Buddy up this expense with a neighbor having a sale on the same weekend. You'll bring her business and vice versa, because people want to hit two or three garage sales in one stop.

The Sign Make an attractive sign that is legible and catches the eye. Use red or blue permanent marker on a white poster board and attach a balloon to the sign. Yours will stand out among *common* signs, and people are more likely to remember your address. Have a sign at high traffic areas in your neighborhood, at each end of your street, and in front of your house—each with a balloon attached.

Legalities If your city or housing area requires a garage sale permit in order to conduct a sale, apply for one. There is usually a very small fee, if any. Some cities only require a completed registration form.

Price It Mark everything ahead of time and categorize your wares as much as possible. Make sure prices are clearly visible. If you're having the sale with a friend, use different colored price stickers to keep the money straight. DO NOT throw everything out in the yard without a price sticker.

If you don't price your wares, you require people to ask how much each and every item costs. They'll either get tired of asking and leave, or they'll buy less.

Generally speaking, you should mark things from 10 to 50 percent of the original price of the item, depending on its condition. People expect to negotiate at a yard sale, so be prepared. Usually there's not as much negotiation at the beginning of the day as there is at the end.

If you don't feel comfortable selling the item at a lower price, then hold firm on your price and ask the person to come back later in the day if he still wants to negotiate. Just as you have to feel good about the price you *pay* at someone else's garage sale, you have to feel good about the price you *get* at yours.

Cash Have enough change on hand to get started. You should have at the very minimum $20 in coins, $20 in one-dollar bills, and $20 in five-dollar bills. Get a good container for your money and don't leave it unattended. Every $50 or so, take the bigger bills into a safe place in the house.

Unless you know the person, don't ever take a check. My parents once sold a set of bunk beds for $200 and helped the folks load them on the truck; the check bounced!

Hold It Don't hold items for people—unless they've already paid for them. The most sincere-looking person may not come back, and you've lost the potential to sell it. Experienced garage-salers do not expect you to hold the item—but they may ask anyway.

If the person has paid for a large item and wants to come back at a later time, put a small sold sign on it and leave it in the yard. It will continue to attract customers to the great bargains you have at your sale.

Clean It You'll get twice the money if your things are clean. Run heavy plastic toys through the dishwasher, put products in their original boxes, hang up as many clothes as you can. I've heard of some folks who shop other garage sales, clean and repair the stuff, and sell it for two to three times as much at their own sales. That's not a garage sale—that's a business!

Marketing Just as grocery and department stores use marketing strategies to sell their goods, you too should think about your marketing plan. Big items, like furniture and bikes, draw people to the sale. Put these items nearest the road or in a visible place.

Categorize the sizes of your clothing. Place all similar sizes together and, again, hang up as many items as possible. Group similar items together in one spot. A cardboard box of plastic children's hangers is junk. On the other hand, plastic hangers tied neatly together with a ribbon will sell. Rearrange your merchandise on the tables throughout the day, as shoppers usually end up moving things around (jeopardizing your well-planned marketing strategies in the process)!

On more expensive items, you might want to cut a copy of the item from a sale circular or catalog—with the price noted. It reminds customers of the original price of goods and helps move the items off your lawn!

Expand You might want to consider broadening your sale a little. If local ordinances permit, you may want to let your children have a lemonade stand, cookie sale, or hot chocolate, coffee, and doughnut stand in conjunction with your garage sale. In the morning the hot drinks will go well; at midmorning and afternoon the cookies and cold drinks will sell. Price these as follows: 25 cents for two medium-size cookies and 25 cents for a small cup of coffee or lemonade; hot cocoa or soda pop goes for 50 cents each, and doughnuts for 50 cents each.

Be sure the child is responsible enough to handle money. It's a wonderful opportunity to teach children financial principles. Make sure they have a money box, adequate change, extra cups and napkins, and an ample supply of product on hand. Put two to three cookies in plastic lunch bags. Set up a trash can by the stand for empties. One of our regular stops in the Fort Drum garage sales was a perpetual weekly sale with hot chocolate and Samoan donuts—greasy, but oh, so good.

★ ★ ★

Whatever your motivation for saving money, you've seen from this chapter that it doesn't have to be painful; in fact, it can be downright *fun*. It's a good idea to read some of this information with your spouse, so you'll be in agreement when you start doing things that may appear to be out of the norm—like coming home with twelve bottles of shampoo (that you got for free!). You'll create a brighter future for your family by paying attention to the little expenses in life. Otherwise, these "little" things can add up to big debt that will only bring stress and strife to you and your spouse.

Remember: A penny saved is *more* than a penny earned!

★ ★ ★

You spend a billion here and a billion there. Sooner or later it adds up to real money.

   —SENATOR EVERETT DIRKSON

    Quoted in *Tale of the Tardy Oxcart* by Chuck Swindoll

★ PROFILE: ★

Name: Wendy Wendler

Spouse's Name: TSgt Tom Wendler

Branch of Service: USAF

Kids: Austin and Taylor

Number of Moves: 11

Years in Service: 14

Work: WW Wonderworks Interior Design, Pure Herb, Ltd. distributor, Birth Buddy Doula Support vice-president, Women's Ministry director, course coordinator for Home Room (Home school group)

Hobbies: scuba-diving, quilting, sewing, painting, gardening, reading, performing arts

Least Favorite Aspect of Military Life: not having a home to call my own for more than a few years and moving away from friends

Favorite Aspect of Military Life: ability to meet new people and touch their lives for the better, and seeing all the world God has created by moving to and visiting different places

CHAPTER FIFTEEN

Hidden Hero Portrait—
Wendy Wendler
A Scuba-Diving Sheriff Conquers Spain

*O*nce a cop, always a cop.

Granted, she wasn't your typical cop. I mean, when a crook looks down a gun barrel, he doesn't expect to see violet eyes with thick black lashes at the other end. When you add lovely raven hair to the mix, the bad guy would probably expect Elizabeth Taylor with a glass of champagne—not James Bond with a .45 magnum.

Deputy Sheriff Wendy Wendler sounds like the lead in a Peter Pan remake, but that's her real name and don't let the doll-like eyes fool you, she's no pushover. Not everyone who meets her believes that, but she can be convincing. Very convincing. Some guys find that out the hard way.

Wendy married Tom, who left his job as a city policeman to become an Air Force Airman, and they moved to Torrejon Air Base in Spain, where he had a unique assignment in downtown Madrid. It was expensive to live downtown, but Wendy said, "I learned to invent tasty meals on a small budget and I became a great baker." This proved to be a skill that served her well later in life when she made cakes as a part-time job.

But there were a few more surprises to be had in Spain. Their car was stolen within the first month. "Welcome to Europe," she thought. It was recovered two days later—sans the radio and tires.

Her main concern was "How are we going to see all of Europe on an airman's salary? I wanted to see every nook and cranny of France, Spain, Italy, England, and Germany that we could cram into our two-year tour." Her ability to stretch a peseta came into play in the form of two backpacks, a Eurail pass, and the adventuresome spirit of a cop. They took fifteen days to see Frankfurt and Munich, Germany; Innsbruck, Austria; and Florence, Italy; Switzerland, Paris, the Riviera, and Costa Brava. It's been said, "If you leave an overseas tour without being in the hole on leave—you're doing something wrong." Tom and Wendy were determined to "not do anything wrong" on that tour.

They rode the rails to castles, cathedrals, and craftsmen. They ate Parisian pastries, Italian escargot, and German chocolate. They saw gypsies and royal gems, museums and monks, and hostels and horses. It was a tour that almost went off without a proverbial hitch.

At one point during the tour, Tom's dad and stepmom joined them in Italy and were anxious to see some of the country. The two couples were in the train station in Rome when a pair of professional crooks approached them. One man asked directions of the men, and he slowly drew them away from Wendy, who was propped up against a brick wall. Behind her back was the video camera that she was holding in place with her body. Distracted by the action in front of her, she moved slightly, but her professional training made her aware that a hand was v-e-r-y slowly reaching in for the camera behind her back.

There was a quick motion as the thief tried to snatch the prize and quickly run away with his booty. But he wasn't prepared for something that happened more swiftly than his ability to escape. Wendy's instincts took over as she reached out, grabbed the thief by the arm, pinned him up against the wall, and began to twist his arm with her strong hand. His eyes bulged in terror under her startlingly strong grip, as he couldn't believe a woman had caught him in this way. He dropped the camera in the pain of her power hold. She bent down to retrieve it, lest the other thief snatch it away. As she did, she loosened her grip long enough for the criminal to break free and run. And he ran and he ran and he ran. . . .

Wendy looked up to see other train passengers with their jaws dropped open as they witnessed "Jane Bond" in action. She smiled, looked at the Spaniards in the crowd, and said in fluent Spanish, "Si eres policia una vez, siempre seras un policia." Which means, "Once a cop, always a cop."

★   ★   ★

Wendy is an amazing individual. She's profiled in this section on balanced budgets because she's learned to be the master of a balanced budget on an enlisted salary in an expensive world. She's as tough on where her money goes as she was on that video camera thief. She's also learned to be resourceful by bringing money into her home using her varied talents.

But she also has a lot of courage, which is evidenced in her hobbies: she was a semi-pro softball player for four years, and she is an avid scuba diver. She conquered her claustrophobia by going into a cavern on one memorable dive. She said she felt water in her mouth, and the next time she breathed, it was all water! She was thirty-two feet down, and all she could think about was that she wouldn't see her little girls again. She remembers, "It scared me, and I wondered how Tom would raise my children without me. Then I heard the voice of my instructor in my head. I fell back on my training by throwing my mouthpiece to the bottom of the cavern and replacing it with my back-up regulator. I purged the valve and began to breathe.

"When I swam out of the cave and surfaced, I was truly shaken with my brush with death—particularly when my girls came running up to me. Boy, was I glad to be back! But I dived again, and I continue to enjoy the beauty and adventure of the exciting sport."

That about sums up Wendy's philosophy of life—when experiencing some of the challenges she's been through, she just dives into life again and keeps trying until it works out beautifully. She sent her husband into harm's way in Somalia for six months when her first child was five months old. While he was gone to Cuba, she was home with a toddler and a baby, and she experienced an emergency situation when a degenerative disk disease rendered her bedridden for two weeks.

Wendy is not only cautious, tough, and savvy, but she's also very much in touch with her feminine side. Her entrepreneurial spirit helps her family financially as she dives into areas that interest her—but they also have a dual function in that they usually help others as well. She has a business called "WWWonderworks" in which she shares her expertise in interior design, and it houses her herb business as well. Her tips have been published in national books as she creatively shows families how to do more with less.

Wendy's most recent endeavor is that of a doula. The word *doula* comes from the Greek word for the most important female slave or servant in an ancient Greek household: the woman who probably helped the lady of the house through her childbearing. The word has come to refer to "a woman experienced in childbirth, who provides continuous physical, emotional, and informational support to the mother before, during, and just after childbirth" (Klaus, Kennell, and Klaus, *Mothering the Mother*). The acceptance of doulas in maternity care is growing rapidly with the recognition of their important contribution to the well-being of mothers and infants.

Wendy has not been hindered by the military lifestyle, as is evident in her choices in life. She faces life as a marathon race, not a 100-yard dash. In doing so, she takes the circumstances she's been dealt, cuts the dead weight, and presses forward with her goals. Along the way, she touches the lives of everyone she meets. Of course, if you're a video camera thief, you probably wouldn't want to meet up with Wendy. She's definitely the kind of homeland hero you would want on *your* side in a fight.

Wendy is a lot like many of you reading this profile in that she would never call herself a hero for rising to the financial and geographical challenges of the military lifestyle. But that is the point exactly: You are a hero because of the sacrifices you so willingly make without a thought for your own desires or comfort. Which of us would *choose* to move, as Wendy has, eleven times in fourteen years? You'll notice a recurring theme in these profiles in that the most difficult part of military life is leaving friends when you move. But Wendy and many of the people reading this page do it on a regular basis. It's not easy, but you keep going anyway.

There's the phrase that is repeated when a family member is presented with a flag upon the death of a loved one: "On behalf of a grateful nation, we thank you." About 25 percent of our nation remembers this. During war, or events like 9/11, that same nation rises boldly in its support of our military and their families. But it is by and large the military families—not only the spouses, but the kids, moms, dads, sisters, and brothers, who must keep this gratitude alive and consistent for the military member. You lead the way in this fight by living out a life of sacrifice and support for your family and spouse, and in doing so, you serve a grateful nation.

★ ★ ★

Take your corner of the world and enjoy each day you are given; you never know what your next adventure might be.
—WENDY WENDLER

Celebrating
Memories

CHAPTER SIXTEEN

Operation Hearts Apart
Creative Coping During Military Separations

~

*B*ob and I had just found out that in Bob's next assignment he was going to fly the snazziest jet on the block—the F-117A Stealth Fighter, or the "Nighthawk." We were excited about this opportunity and looked forward to moving back to see our friends in New Mexico.

One Sunday a few weeks before the move, I opened the Sunday paper to search for the coupon inserts, and my eyes fell on a startling headline: "Stealth Shot Down in Kosovo." The photo showed a charred heap of twisted metal—all that remained of the type of jet my husband was to fly.

I took the paper to Bob, stuffed it under his nose, and asked, "I thought they couldn't see you in a Stealth!"

Bob shrugged his shoulders and said, "Well, the pilot was all right."

It just goes to show that even a $50-million jet can have a bad day. As a matter of fact, when Bob went to train in that weapon system, he landed the jet, and the parachute came out just fine, when suddenly a gust of wind wrapped the chute around the jet. This little weather mishap caused almost $45,000 in damage.

Whether we fly jets, drive cars, or live in a house full of kids—spills, scrapes, and boo-boos happen. And these events always seem to happen when the guys go on temporary duty (TDY).

It's the unspoken TDY rule: Almost as soon as our spouse pulls out of the driveway to serve God and country, something or someone will break down.

I think the Kays have had more than their fair share of these "events." Even though I have hundreds of examples of Kay Family Mishaps, let me share just a couple.

Ever since lipstick was invented in Cleopatra's time, there have been little King Tuts and princesses who insist on exploring the various uses of makeup. When Bethany was eighteen months old, I found her in front of my bathroom mirror, sitting on the sink, experimenting with my red lipstick. She'd taken a new tube and smeared it ALL OVER her ENTIRE face. Her cheeks, forehead, nose, and chin were covered in big globs of lipstick. When I discovered her, she was trying to wipe it off her face—with my white cashmere sweater!

Then there was the time I took the five children on a home-school field trip to the doughnut factory. Joshua was a newborn, sleeping in the stroller. Jonathan was strapped on my back in a pack, and the other three children were within arm's reach. Jonathan fussed and grumped because he wanted to be in on the action on the floor, but he soon quieted down. About thirty minutes into the tour, I discovered the reason Jonathan was so quiet.

His perch on my back was just the right height to have his pick of chocolate-filled doughnuts on the cooling rack. He'd grabbed several and stuffed them in his lap and then ate them as needed. He was such a thoughtful baby that he decided to share (it runs in the family). He found a fellow toddler, who was also perched on his mother's backpack, and soon the two were exchanging doughnuts (behind their moms' backs). By the time I felt something wet and sticky on my neck, it was too late. I ended up with chocolate-covered hair—and a happy but very hyperactive toddler.

★ ★ ★

Whether you are separated from your spouse due to travel, work situations, or military duties, it's important to stay connected while you're apart. Separation is such a regular part of the military family's lifestyle, it is easy to get buried under the busyness and forget to take purposeful steps toward staying connected. There's a tendency to get so caught up in the woes of single parenting and endless "messes" that we forget the responsibility we have to ourselves, our spouse, and our kids to stay in touch.

Another problem that arises when families are geographically split is that household budgets may get sidetracked, and the family gets into serious financial trouble in the process. Whether the separation is twelve days or twelve months, here are some practical and inexpensive ways to keep the home fires burning—even if it's from five thousand miles away.

Before They Go

There are some meaningful things you can do before your spouse leaves that will help you stay connected throughout the departure. Here are a few ideas to get your creative juices flowing:

Notes-to-Go Depending upon how long they're gone, send a bundle of notes with them. If they're gone for three months, make them weekly notes with a special memory, a word of encouragement, or a funny cartoon. You'll also be sending them e-mails and snail mail letters, but this bundle will give your spouse a sense of taking a bit of you (and the kids) with him.

Watch Out for Fireworks Part of the classic "Pre-TDY" syndrome is that each person begins to emotionally separate himself/herself for what lies ahead. Expect the tensions to be high and be on guard for potential fireworks over the littlest things. Simply being aware of these emotions and potential disagreements can go a long way toward diffusing the situation.

Letters/Gifts/Flowers With Friends One thing the service member can do before his/her departure is to leave letters and gifts with friends of yours—to be distributed each week. Or, they can arrange for flowers to be delivered on key dates. This bit of forethought means the world to the one(s) left behind. Make sure to see the Wish List at the end of this chapter for some great ideas.

Family Photos This is a good idea no matter how long or short the TDY or deployment. Get a good family photo and put it in a sturdy frame with a stand of its own. I even take one of these photos with me when I travel for business and speaking engagements. I show it to people on the airplane (especially men that want to get my phone number—nothing like a photo of seven children to scare them away!). Have your spouse place the photo in the hotel room or barracks as a reminder of two things: (1) his actions today will affect his family tomorrow, and (2) there's someone counting on him at home. When I travel, I like to place the photo by the television as a reminder to watch shows that will feed my mind and spirit rather than make my brain cells dry up!

Videotaping Memories Jody Dale, Army chaplain wife, says, "About a week before Garry went to Somalia, we gathered as a family in the kids' bedrooms, and Garry read stories to them while I ran the video camera. I captured their faces, the pre-bedtime prayers, and even some of the songs they sang with their daddy. We watched the video while he was gone and still do, occasionally, even to this day. Each time we watch, it makes us thankful he came home."

Taping Stories If you have young children, consider making an audio-cassette tape of the deployed parent reading their favorite stories. Army Chaplain Egert recorded stories and family devotions before he left so his children could hear him read nightly. Even young babies will benefit from hearing that parent's voice, and upon their return will adapt more easily because they are familiar with that voice. But be prepared to explain that Mommy or Daddy cannot hear them if they talk to the cassette player!

Cards Home There seems to be a gazillion and one things the service member has to do before he or she deploys, and buying cards to send back home can easily get overlooked. Buy some stationery, some cards for kids, or even postcards, and self-address them, including postage (if they'll be near a U.S. military base with a post office). Be sure to have an ample supply of cards for each individual child, because the kids will love receiving this mail.

Investment Consider investing in a camera for your computer as well as one for your spouse so that you can "see" each other over the Internet while you talk and see each other online. Or, you might even consider an investment in a digital video camera that will allow you to send both stills and moving footage to your spouse (or vice versa if you want to let them take the camera over and if it's allowed by the regulation in their deployed area). You might even want to consider investing in a mobile e-mail unit so your spouse will not be dependent on getting to a computer and a line in order to "talk" to you. Once again, you will have to verify that the deployed installation commander allows such devices.

Phone Cards Buy a renewable, prepaid calling card for your spouse; they have special ones for overseas, and this could greatly reduce long-distance calling expenses.

Follow the List There is a pre-deployment briefing that your spouse is required to attend. They will bring home documents, such as power-of-attorney and notification paper work. Be sure you take the time to go over these with your spouse and make plans accordingly. You will find a more detailed list in the next chapter.

While They Are Gone

E-mail, Cards, and Letters If you don't have e-mail, set up a free account through *www.yahoo.com* or *www.hotmail.com.* Even remote military assignments very often have access to e-mail. This is an excellent way to tell your loved one about your day and to ask questions and advice. Be sure you reread your letters before you send them, especially if you're venting or feeling sad when you write. This kind of correspondence tends to be one-dimensional and will often communicate a tone or message that you regret once you are in a better frame of mind. Remember to be honest and yet keep your notes as positive as possible. Proverbs 25:25 says, *"Like cold water to a weary soul, so is good news from a distant land."* Do jabber on about the day, the routine, what you did—these things seem meaningless to you but are part of the fiber of life that your mate is likely missing and looking forward to upon his return.

Routines It's important to stick with your normal routine as much as possible, especially if you have children. When your spouse is away, there's a tendency to order pizza every night, let the house go, and allow the children to break bedtime curfews. But consistency will keep you on track and give your children the stability that can only come with a regular schedule.

Top Twelve Don'ts for Deployment

I asked a database of military families for their input in much of this book, which provides a diversity of interests and ideas. Quite a few of them came up with important "Don'ts."

1. *Don't have a negative attitude*; it will hurt you, your kids, and everyone who is unfortunate enough to be around you!
2. *Don't spend time alone with other men*; establish boundaries during this particularly vulnerable time.
3. *Don't listen to your favorite love songs* or romantic movies if it makes you nostalgic for your mate. Instead, watch a comedy with a friend.
4. *Don't buy big-ticket items* without your spouse's approval—no matter how depressed you are!
5. *Don't give in to impulse buying* on the smaller-ticket items either; they will surely add up to big debts!
6. *Don't clean out your spouse's "stuff,"* even if he never does listen to those eight-track tapes!
7. *Don't stay home alone*—especially if you have little ones. Join a MOPS (Mothers of Preschoolers) in your area. For more information on attending or starting a MOPS group in your area, go to *www.gospelcom.net/mops/index.shtml* or call 1-800-929-1287.
8. *Don't turn down offers for help.* Take people up on their offers to take you to lunch, come over for dinner, baby-sit

your kids (if you trust them), and even bring you a casserole. Now is the time to accept help!

9. *Don't overdose on news shows,* especially when your spouse is involved in a "hot news" conflict. Don't let your kids hear much (if any) of the news involving your spouse's deployment. Madeline Brazell says, "Andrew, who was only two when Duane went to Desert Storm, started to exhibit disturbing behavior during the first days of the war when we kept the news on almost all day."

10. *Don't overdo it on TV in general*—too much of it makes your brain turn to mush and your morals turn maudlin.

11. *Don't use TV, videos, DVDs, computers, or game systems as a baby-sitter.* Limit their use to one show or one hour a day, and your child will have a better outlook on life.

12. *Don't list your physical address in the phone book or on any registration information.* When a Stealth went down in Kosovo, and they didn't know who the pilot was, CNN was standing curbside at every pilot's house listed in the phone book!

The list continues for the "do's" while they're gone.

Build Something! Leigh Ann Trevillion is a mother of two-year-old twins, whose husband travels frequently. She's an unusual gal who likes to ride live bulls, go skydiving, and hang from the top of the 100-foot skeleton of a construction site. Therefore, her method of coping while her husband is gone may or may not fit your personality. She says, "My way of getting through is to take on building projects to surprise him with on his return. . . . I've built a room addition, painted a room a new color, and built a storage shed."

Enjoy the Down Time Jill Mingear, Army spouse, says, "My husband, Darren, was gone at least one week per month when we were stationed at Fort Campbell, Kentucky. I worked, and we had one child at the time. I actually enjoyed the down time of less laundry, cooking, and a lightened schedule."

Independence Day The truth is, if you are highly dependent upon your spouse for your emotional well-being, your ability to explore new things, or your happiness in general, you're going to have a harder time of it. Military spouses learn to be flexible, and this characteristic is never more needed than when the unit is deployed or they are TDY. Jill Mingear puts it well: "When the boys were preschoolers, I'd plan a trip home to see my family. I would take all kinds of road trips. If I had waited for Darren to take me everywhere—I never would have gone *anywhere!*"

New Adventures While routines are important to families, it doesn't mean you have to exclude new adventures. Try taking the kids snow-skiing, castle hopping (if you're stationed in Europe), and exploring your geographical part of the world. The kids can tell the deployed parent about their "adventures," and when they are exploring fun, new areas, they are less likely to feel they are "missing" life.

Installation Resources Every military base, regardless of the branch of service, has programs and resources for the families of deployed military members. Make sure you take advantage of these! Depending upon the base and the program, perks can include everything from free oil changes to regular audiovisual telephone calls, where your entire family can talk with your spouse at a prearranged time.

Extended Family While it's important to visit extended family, especially during deployments of three months or more, it's also important to keep a balance on these visits. It's very easy to shift the *interdependence* that exists between a husband and wife to a *dependence* upon extended family. Your real home is where "the military sends you" or where your *nuclear* family—your spouse and kids—is. If you're visiting your parents' home during each deployment and calling that "home," the potential to depend on *extended family* more than your *nuclear family* could possibly under-mine that primary family relationship. Jill Mingear says, "I feel it is important to get away from the post when the spouse is deployed, but if you make a habit of running to your parents every time your spouse deploys, that can be unhealthy. You have to be independent for yourself and your spouse's sake. They don't need to worry about things falling apart on the home front."

Gifts Sometimes your friends or parents may want to help *you* by buying special gifts or treats. They will sometimes ask you what you want or need. Give them a copy of this book and direct them to this section. Suggested gift items are: phone cards, movie tickets, restaurant gift certif-icates, free baby-sitting, magazine subscriptions, and humorous books or inspirational books (I like anything by Becky Freeman or Dave Meurer).

Teachers Let your children's teachers know the deployment/TDY sched-ule so they will be aware of potential mood swings or "acting out" in a child who may be missing his/her parent. This helps the teacher to be more understanding without damaging the child's spirit.

Class Projects Consider approaching your kids' teachers and asking if their classmates can use some of the English or writing course time to write letters to the deployed spouse. Your children will be proud of Mommy or Daddy's important job and the fact that others are concerned for their safety as well.

Sticky-Note Fun Madeline Brazell, Air Force spouse, says, "When Duane would leave on a TDY, I would make a calendar and mark off the days until he returned with small sticky notes over the dates. Andrew and Chris were preschoolers, and they enjoyed removing a sticky note each day. I was relieved from being asked constantly how much longer Daddy would be gone!"

If you are particularly crafty, you could take Madeline's idea and make an "advent calendar," marking each day in a special way.

Special Treats I've noticed that when the guys deploy on a mission, some of the wives "treat" themselves in destructive ways. It's the feeling that "I have to do this alone, so I deserve this (fill-in-the-blank.)" If some of those indulgences include overspending on credit cards, over-indulging in comfort foods, or going to questionable places such as nightclubs, then you will not feel better in the long run. Instead of unhealthy outlets, treat yourself to an occasional massage at the massage therapy school or a manicure or pedicure at a cosmetology college. Go out to lunch with an encouraging girl friend (go to my Web site at *www.elliekay.com* for links to restaurant coupons). Take the kids to the dollar theater (or matinee), zoo, museum, or on a nature walk.

Exercise I've always made exercise a priority—even with five kids! The result is that I have more energy, a lifted mood, and better ability to cope with the pressures of being a single mom while Bob is gone. Even a brisk three-mile walk three times a week is enough to keep your body healthy and keep those extra pounds at bay. Try listening to uplifting music while you exercise.

The New You! Madeline Brazell also offered this idea: "Make plans to do those things you never get around to doing while your spouse is at home. Start a new exercise program and surprise him when he returns. Change the color of your bedroom; buy a new pet for your kids (we got small ones like fish or birds). Organize closets, photo albums, recipes, etc. Get in touch with old friends and relatives; start a neighborhood women's Bible study; or have a garage sale." Or buy a new SUV (just kidding)!

Kindred Spirits A kindred spirit is someone you can confide in about virtually anything—fears, temptations, dreams, or desires. I've found that while these true friends are precious and rare, they are also crucial to my emotional health while Bob is flying afar. There's nothing like a friend who has a knack for saying the right thing at the right time.

Gripe-Free Zone Jody Dale, Army chaplain wife, says, "NEVER gripe to your spouse when talking to him/her while he/she is deployed. They can't do anything about it and feel helpless. Take your problems to God and to a good friend. Report the good things, fun events, wishes and hopes for tomorrow. Always let them know they are missed, but not to the point where you are devastated and cannot cope. The truth is—you can!"

Laughter Is Good Medicine Loved ones need to laugh while they are gone, so send pictures, jokes, cartoons, or goofy packages from home while encouraging the deployed member to do the same.

Volunteer This is a fantastic way to take your mind off your loneliness: helping others. Most military-sponsored programs offer childcare reimbursement, so it serves the dual function of providing a break from the kiddies. If your children are school age, consider watching the preschoolers up the street for another mom whose spouse is deployed. Even if you only offered this service once or twice a month, it's a great feeling to give someone else a break.

Anonymous Gifts Brighten the life of the spouse who is having a particularly tough time by leaving or mailing anonymous gifts. For ideas, see the "Wish List" at the end of this chapter.

Homecoming and Reunions

One Family Support director that I spoke with, Lenn Furrow, said, "The best advice I could give the military member who is deployed for a long period of time is: Do not come home early and unannounced. Your spouse has imagined the reunion countless times in her mind, and if you suddenly surprise her a day or a week early, the house will not be as clean as she wanted it to be, your favorite meal won't be prepared, and she might look a sight. Don't rob her of the joy of the homecoming by arriving early and unannounced!"

Pace Yourself Deployment and TDY orders change all the time. Don't zero in on a specific date. Instead, be prepared (as much as you can) to have your spouse call and announce a change in the arrival date (either earlier or later).

Expect the Unexpected During long separations, we women tend to glamorize the reunion, and it's rarely quite as wonderful as it was in our minds. Plan all you want and make it special, but realize that it may not go off exactly the way you wanted it to, and decide ahead of time that it will be all right.

Rough Landings The post-deployment adjustment can be a severe bummer. You've been independent and in charge at home, while your spouse has only been responsible for himself/herself while deployed. Have your spouse read this section so that you will both be prepared for the adjustments that happen upon reunion. The deployed spouse needs to give the homebound spouse room to move from independence back into interdependence. It is best to turn over areas of responsibility slowly. Very slowly. The deployed spouse may feel as if they're just sitting on the sidelines for the first few days, and that is all right. Sometimes it's the best place for them to be as "normalcy" returns to your reunited household.

Special Times The events you've been anticipating for weeks or months are now about to happen. It's important to realize that you don't have to do everything in the first few days that your spouse is home. Consider it a mini-vacation that lasts a couple of weeks. Throughout that time you can: farm out the kids for a night, create a candlelight dinner with favorite foods another night, buy a new outfit for another night (I like *Victoria's Secret* and so does Bob!), or rent a favorite new movie for yet another night.

Extended Family Try to discourage extended family from visiting the first week or two that your spouse is back home. Once again, you can give them their own copy of this book and have them read this section. You deserve some time alone, and you will need the space to adjust to being a family again. Madeline Brazell says, "After Duane was gone four months, some well-meaning relatives wanted to drive down to the base and meet him on the runway. I gently asked them to please wait a week. I was so thankful they understood."

Bonus Section—The Service Member's "Wish Book"

When I was a kid, Sears published a HUGE Christmas "Wish Book" catalog. I remember sitting on the couch, playing a game in which I wished that Santa would give me a gift on each page; all I had to do was choose. You can make it Christmas for your service member any time of the year by creating a "Wish Book." You could send several at once, or create a new "page" each week.

This might even be a good project for your Family Support Group/

Family Readiness Group or your spouse's coffee group. The emphasis can be on either romance or family bonding (or both). Some of these will be items they can use right away, while others hold a promise for the future. You can send a note with a special gift attached or enclosed in the envelope or package. Here are some ideas to get you started:

- I Wish for You . . . Laughter With Friends
  (Write an account of something cute the kids did that week.)
- I Wish for You . . . Beauty for Ashes
  (Something lovely made out of something unusual. The kids once made "angels" out of spray-painted Coke cans that were folded in the center, using the top of the can as the angel's head and the opening as its mouth.)
- I Wish for You . . . Peace & Tranquility
  (A mood music CD with a note that you will be listening to the same music)
- I Wish for You . . . A Special Evening
  (A gift certificate to their favorite restaurant to be redeemed upon their return)
- I Wish for You . . . Health
  (Vitamins or a power nutrition bar)
- I Wish for You . . . Thin Thighs
  (Firming gel or support hose as a gag gift)
- I Wish for You . . . Good Hair Days
  (Any hair-care product, preferably one they use!)
- I Wish for You . . . A Rainbow After the Storm
  (Anything with a rainbow on it, or have the kids draw and color a rainbow)
- I Wish for You . . . Special Moments & Good Memories
  (A photo album—to keep photos they take while they're away as well as the ones you send)
- I Wish for You . . . Good Conversation
  (A phone card)
- I Wish for You . . . Warm Connections
  (Stationery)
- I Wish for You . . . A Breath of Freshness
  (A supply of Altoids or other breath mints)
- I Wish for You . . . Wisdom
  (A book to challenge their mind)

- I Wish for You . . . Love
  (A big chocolate kiss)
- I Wish for You . . . Kodak Moments
  (A disposable camera)
- I Wish for You . . . A Stamp of Approval
  (Stamps)
- I Wish for You . . . Happy Surprises
  (Anything . . . try to make it something they enjoy, and be creative!)
- I Wish for You . . . Light at the End of the Tunnel
  (A candle)
- I Wish for You . . . The Promise of Spring
  (Any bulb plant)
- I Wish for You . . . A Quiet Afternoon
  (Hot cocoa packets)
- I Wish for You . . . Quiet Moments With God
  (A good devotional book, such as *Taking the High Ground* by Col. Jeff O'Leary)
- I Wish for You . . . Romantic Moments in a "Tub for Two"
  (Bubble bath to be brought back home in anticipation of your reunion)
- I Wish for You . . . No Postponed Returns or Extended Moments Apart
  (A travel alarm clock, showing that the time will pass)
- I Wish for You . . . Healthy Competition
  (A game; maybe one they can play with other soldiers on deployment)
- I Wish for You . . . Good Scents
  (Their favorite cologne or the scent *you* usually wear for them to spray on their pillow and remember you by)
- I Wish for You . . . Self-Sufficiency
  (A mini tool kit or Swiss Army knife if you're allowed to send them)
- I Wish for You . . . A Platform for Praise
  (A platform shoe purchased at the local thrift shop as a gag gift)
- I Wish for You . . . Someone to Help You Bear Your Burdens
  (A stuffed Teddy bear)
- I Wish for You . . . Good Therapy
  (Aromatherapy candle or lotion)
- I Wish for You . . . Roses Without Thorns
  (A rose potpourri ball or silk rose, or one drawn by the kids)

- I Wish for You . . . A Clean House
  (Homemade gift certificate guaranteeing a clean house—if they don't arrive early and unannounced!)
- I Wish for You . . . No More "Ring Around the Collar"
  (A bottle of Shout or Spray 'n' Wash spot cleaner)
- I Wish for You . . . No More Headaches
  (Tylenol PM or Excedrin)
- I Wish for You . . . Ageless Beauty
  (A night cream or aftershave lotion)

★   ★   ★

Chuck Swindoll, bestselling author of about a gazillion books, once said, "Words can never adequately convey the incredible impact of our attitude toward life. The longer I live, the more convinced I am that life is 10 percent what happens to us and 90 percent how we respond to it" (*Strengthening Your Grip,* Word Publishing, 1983). This is true for all military families, and it is never truer than when your spouse is gone. There are lots of tips in this section, and even if you learned just a few things, it could make all the difference in the next deployment—because the next one will come, and . . .

It will never be convenient timing.

It will never be short enough.

It will never be over until your spouse separates or retires from the military.

But . . . I don't want to end this important chapter on a negative note. So let's put some perspective on the topic. . . .

Even though the timing isn't perfect, you can make the most of the time.

Even though it's longer than you'd like, it isn't forever.

Even though it's part of military life, you will likely miss some aspects about the lifestyle when you're through.

The most important thing to remember, as much as we joke about "serving your country in Hawaii," is that there is genuine and abiding *purpose* in the service member's going. It's a much bigger perspective than we can imagine, because . . .

If it weren't for their mission, we wouldn't have freedom.

If it weren't for the tears of farewell, we'd never shed tears of a safe homecoming.

If it weren't for your sacrifice at home, we wouldn't have America as we now know it.

Perspective makes all the difference.

CHAPTER SEVENTEEN

Courage Under Fire
Facing Fear With Faith

⁓

*T*here are no guarantees in life—whether you're a fighter pilot or a free-lance writer. But I also know, by faith, that there is a "still, small voice" within us that is the voice of God speaking to the fear within. That is something that will carry us through anything this life throws at us. It isn't always easy, but it can be all right.

I didn't learn that lesson as soon as I fell off the Air Force turnip truck. It took me a while to realize how to cope with the dangers and uncertainties of the profession my husband chose. When we dated, Bob shrugged off his dangerous profession by saying, "Hey, I fly jets, and it sure beats working for a living!"

I remember the day I learned how dangerous it really was . . . it was a baptism by fire.

Bob had been back in the Air Force for a few months. My sunny California afternoon was rudely interrupted by an urgent knock on the front door. There stood my next-door neighbor, Michelle, with tears running down her face and panic in her voice.

"Did you hear?" she sobbed. "A jet went down this afternoon. Have you heard from Bob?" One of the jets had crashed, and the squadron automatically went on "shut down" status. There was no communication going into or out of the squadron. All the wives had to wait the agonizing hours until the crash was confirmed and the aviator's next of kin notified.

So I waited.

We all did.

We had no choice.

I wondered if the wing commander's car with the ominous white roof

and General's star would drive up to my house, accompanied by the chap-
lain, for the "notification" process.

For six hours we all waited.

The white-topped car drove to the house of a young nurse with a three-
week-old baby girl. Dave Campbell was dead.

★ ★ ★

From then on, Bob and I had a code we used for accidents. Before
the squadron would go on "shut down," if he had any chance at all, he
would call and say, "Hi, I had a good flight, and I love you. Good-bye."
Then he would abruptly hang up.

He made that call too many times, but the fact that he was the one
calling meant that he *wasn't* the one in the "jet gone down."

I think it's a blessing the way memories from those harrowing days
fade as we veterans on the home front keep moving forward in this life
we call "the service." But it only takes another phone call for the past to
thrust its ugly face into our conscious mind and come rushing forward
again.

I got that call—two nights ago.

Bob was night flying, and he *never* calls home when he flies that late.
I was working on this manuscript. At 10:30 P.M. the phone rang. I
checked the caller ID , which said it was "unavailable." If it were the base,
there would be another prefix. I answered the phone to hear Bob's voice:

"Hi. I wanted to let you know I had a good flight, and I love you.
Good-bye." Click. The line went dead.

My mind raced as my memory was shaken out of complacency—the
"take it for granted" mode I easily fall into when it hasn't happened in a
while. I thought about how earlier this month Bob was at an air show at
the Navy base of Point Mugu, and an F-4 went down during the show,
erupting into a fireball in full view of the spectators. The Navy pilot and
weapons officer were instantly killed. What made it worse was that it was
a home air show, so their deaths were witnessed by dozens of friends,
peers, and family.

Had that only happened this month? How did I forget about it so
quickly? I thought to myself. My mind shifted into autopilot as I quickly
processed Bob's message:

> *It was our code for a jet gone down.*
> *This means a jet has crashed.*

> *The caller ID was "unavailable," which means he wasn't call-*
> *ing from the base.*
> *Are they off site; did it happen over a different airspace?*
> *Will he even be home tonight?*
> *He could be gone for hours, or even days, if the circumstances*
> *are quirky.*
> *I think the Stealths are the only jets in the area that fly at*
> *night . . . I think.*
> *This means that it was likely another Stealth.*
> *This means I will probably know the pilot—and his wife.*
> *Almost all the guys are married with children.*
> *It wasn't Bob, and I'm relieved about that.*
> *But it was someone else's husband, someone else's son, someone*
> *else's daddy.*
> *Was it Phil? No, he's DNIF and not flying this week.*
> *Was it Clint? Oh no! Myra has three preschoolers!*
> *No . . . relief! Clint wasn't flying because of his recent surgery.*
> *Was it Lynn's husband? She's about to pop with baby number*
> *three any day now.*

And so my mind went down its checklist. Thinking the worst-case scenario and the best—which was only slightly better than the worst. For fifty-five minutes I sat there . . . wondering . . . knowing I would get the "wives' rumor mill" running if I called even one other pilot's wife. I wouldn't do that. I didn't do that.

So I sat.

And I waited.

And I thought.

But I didn't cry.

And I didn't panic.

Because I'd been through this before.

When the phone rang again at 11:25, I was relieved to hear Bob's voice; at least I would *know* something.

"It was a German plane, a Toronado. They fly at night, like we do, and they do lots of low-level stuff. I was flying above them and watched as they crashed into a mountain and erupted into a fireball. The crash started a forest fire. I don't see how either the pilot or the backseater could have survived.

"I called you from the crew chief's cell phone as soon as I landed, because I wasn't sure it wasn't one of ours—and they could possibly shut down the squadron by the time I walked the line."

My first reaction was one that later made me feel guilty: *I was relieved.*

Relieved that it wasn't my husband, my friend's husband, or our squadron.

Relieved we wouldn't have to sit through another friend's memorial service.

Relieved we wouldn't have another event to compartmentalize, only to be awakened by a future phone call.

Relieved that I wouldn't have to live through the emotional gymnastics of looking into the face of a widowed friend, trying to come up with *anything* that didn't sound like a mindless platitude.

I was ashamed of my humanity.

But . . . we must all cope with this life as best we can. In our own way. Different for each person. Good, bad, and indifferent.

"Good" it wasn't us.

"Bad" it was someone without a name or a face I knew.

And because of the latter, I had become "indifferent."

But Bob had to fly again the next day and the day after that.

And I'm a good pilot's wife.

So just as he compartmentalized the accident, so do I.

I drive the kids to school the next morning, I pick them up in the afternoon, and life goes on—for my family and me.

For the German wife and mother three blocks up the street . . .

Life has suddenly stopped.

★   ★   ★

Sending a spouse on a deployment, out on a ship or to the field, is hard enough, but sending them into harm's way is doubly difficult. Military spouses cope with these life-and-death situations as a matter of course, but that doesn't mean it is easy. There are some practical "housekeeping" issues you can take care of to make sure your affairs are in order, and I've listed those below. However, even more important are the emotional, psychological, and spiritual preparations that can make the difference between your personal success or failure as you handle these critical issues.

Some of the greatest personal growth I've seen in myself and in my friends has occurred during a time of extended separation. Listen to how other military spouses have coped:

A Remote Experience

Patti Wickre, wife of TSgt. Tom Wickre, says, "A remote experience not only affects the person going on the remote assignment. The spouse left behind feels remote from everyone else. All our friends' spouses are still at home. You feel like you are intruding if you do anything with them as a family. You feel left out. In many ways this past year without Tom has been a remote experience for me despite having friends and family around."

When Tom called Patti to tell her that he got a solo assignment to Korea, she immediately began to sob—an activity that almost became routine in the weeks to follow. She said, "I knew this was a possibility before I married him, and I married him anyway." As a graduate of the U.S. Coast Guard Academy, she thought she was pretty well prepared for the military lifestyle choice—but that was before her husband got orders to Korea and left her behind with two preschoolers.

She went through the typical roller coaster emotions. She said, "Tom would do something that frustrated me, and I'd just wish he was already gone. Then I'd feel absolutely terrible for even thinking that."

After he left, she admits that she was in pretty bad shape for a while. The turning point for Patti was when she thought about how she had the kids, her home, her own bed, while he was truly ALONE. No family. No wife. No one at all. It wasn't easy for her, but she realized that it was harder for her husband in some ways.

Once she came to this watershed moment, she decided to take charge of their months of separation. The kids built a chain, counting down the days until his mid-tour break. Each link was for a week. They would remove the link from their chain at home and write down everything they did that week on it. Then they would mail it to Tom, and he assembled it in his room. As theirs was getting smaller, Tom's was getting longer, and he felt like he was still part of their lives. She started applying many of the "Hearts Apart" ideas suggested in our previous chapter. She participated in the base's official "Hearts Apart" program and found a network of other women whose spouses had deployed, as well as the "Give Parents a Break" program at the local Family Support Center.

But Patti said the most important thing she did for herself during the separation was to take the time to look into issues of her personal faith. She says, "With about sixty days to go on the tour, I was finishing up a Bible study on conversations. There was a verse in there that really spoke to my heart. It was Isaiah 50:4: 'The Lord has given me an instructed tongue so that I may know the word to sustain the weary.' My neighbor told me that someday I would be a comfort to someone else who was going through the same thing. Sure enough, an acquaintance came up to me in church and said they'd just found out her husband was going remote. I started to cry, and I will be here for them when he leaves."

Even though they were trying times, Patti gained strength she never knew she had. She concludes her story by saying, "It's a time for growth. God has shown me so much within myself as a person, a mother, and a wife of a military member. I'm proud to be a military spouse. It's difficult, but there's no other man I'd rather be beside than my husband, Tom."

Conquering Fear

Joyce Edwards, wife of Chief MSgt. James A. Edwards, had a hard time when her husband went from being a mechanic on an F-86 aircraft unit to being a flight engineer. His first trip was the worst, and they were stationed at Dobbins Air Force Base. She had two young children, and she said, "My mind began racing and anxiety filled me as I thought of his itinerary and all the taking off and landing. I was consumed with 'what ifs?' I made myself and our children miserable!"

When James came home, he had a big smile on his face, looking handsome in his flight suit and eager to share all the wonderful places he had been and what he'd seen. Suddenly Joyce had her watershed moment, as she realized that all her worry and fears were totally useless. In no way could they change her husband's situation or his safety, and they only made her feel miserable. Just like Patti, she had a friend from the base chapel share a verse that had deep meaning for her: "The angel of the Lord encamps around them that fear him, and delivers them" (Psalm 34:7). Her friend told her that in the original language of Hebrew that word *encamps* literally means "the angels digging a trench around the borders of your property, and nothing can cross the boundaries that belong to you without God's divine permission."

From then on, Joyce says, "I imagined the angels around my husband, and it gave me peace." Her husband went on to accumulate 10,000 flying hours, flying in Viet Nam, Desert Storm, and many other missions. He retired in 1992, and they have been married forty-three years. She never regretted her decision to trust God with her husband's safety.

You're Not Falling Apart!

There may be times when the pressure of the firefight gets to you, and you think you're falling apart! But you're not. No, you're really not.

We all feel that way at times, and that's when we need a strong faith and a good friend. If you don't have a strong faith, then now would be a good time to explore that aspect of your spirituality through the resources listed in this book—starting as near as your installation's chapel. An Army spouse said, "Sad days will come, but that does not mean you are falling apart. Recognize them for what they are. Use those days to appreciate all that you have, for the sadness comes due to the fact that you are missing someone special. You can be thankful you have someone to miss. Memories of our loved ones affect us, and that is a good thing."

Wendy, an Air Force spouse whose husband was sent to Somalia when she had a new baby, said, "Be confident in who you are when your spouse leaves. Some women feel that they are not capable of many things that their husbands normally handle. Look deep inside yourself. You can handle anything they can, and if not, you can find someone to help out. Look to your unit, friends, or church for the help you need. You may not know this, but the military trains you in a strange way for many obstacles that most civilians do not understand and could not handle."

Of Death and Dying

We saw in the earlier story of this chapter that pilots learn to compartmentalize death in order to do their jobs. This is true of soldiers and sailors as well. If your spouse goes into a dangerous situation and experiences war and death, they will be forever changed. But not all change is bad. One of the things that comforted me when I was a new bride was the peace that comes from knowing where Bob would go if he were to die. At PWOC, I went to a study on the names of God and it changed the way I viewed God. One wife who sent her husband into such a situation said, "Be aware that your spouse will never be the same person after being faced with war and death. You must allow him to slowly reenter the world you live in. Things will be different for them, and they may not talk about it. Don't push them by always asking 'why?' In their own time they will open up."

If you have a spouse who has been involved in life-and-death situations, there are counseling programs at your local chapel or Family Support Center equivalent to help the service member as well as the family. Brig. Gen. Dick Abel (Ret) said, "Different situations can be a springboard to spiritual growth." Take advantage of these early in the situation. If your spouse is overseas and involved in war and death, visit the counseling center before they get home so that a trained professional can tell you what to expect and how you can make reentry easier on your spouse.

One important aspect of reentry after such a dramatic experience is for the spouse not to turn over responsibilities too quickly to the returning service member. It needs to be a slow transition, and sometimes certain activities trigger painful memories for them. No matter how innocuous the activity seems, it may be something they simply cannot handle for a while, or ever. It could be something as simple as reading a child's favorite storybook that reminds them of how their friend who died read to his kids. Or a trip to the zoo could trigger a memory of where a fellow fallen soldier used to work as a second job. Be sensitive to your spouse, whether the issues make sense to you or not. That is why counseling is very important for both parties after a combat situation.

Chapel Programs

Pray, Pray, Pray

There is a diversity of faiths among military families, but most people find comfort in prayer regardless of their religious affiliation. Prayer can actually lower blood pressure, release tension, and contribute to an individual's mental, emotional, and physical health. Give your family this incredible gift by setting up a regular time in the morning (to start your day) or evening (to prepare for the long nights) for prayer. Let your spouse know that you are all praying for him or her; you might even consider praying for the same things on the same nights to create a feeling of unity.

Jody Dale, wife of an Army chaplain, said this about her husband's tour in Somalia: "My strength was my prayer group and knowing to Whom I was praying. Friends who truly cared and prayed made me get involved and get out to the gym. I had a friend, Judy, who insisted that I get moving when I least felt like it. At times I was so mean to her and unthankful, but as I look back, she helped me keep my mind and body active, and our friendship was strengthened."

Defending the Military Marriage

This is an outstanding program currently available to military members through the HomeBuilders Couples Series (*www.homebuilders.com*). The topics include: "Basic Training," "Communicating in the Trenches," "More-Month-Than-Money Blues," and "SEAL Training: Sexual Accountability and Love."

For more information on these time-friendly studies, call 1-800-444-

6006 Ext. 286 or go to *www.milmin.com.* This inexpensive study book was written by Lt. Col. Jim Fishback, USA (Ret.) and his wife, Bea. It is a short course that you go through with other couples to help strengthen your marriage before those "trial by fire" situations occur.

Catholic and Protestant Women of the Chapel—Other Programs

These are only a couple of the military-sponsored programs that offer assistance to those who are seeking a deeper faith. Bible studies, religious education programs for kids, youth groups, summer vacation Bible School, chapel services for all denominations, and spiritual counseling are all as close as your nearest installation chapel.

Tape Resources—Focus on the Family
www.family.org or 1-800-A-FAMILY

The Army Family CS116—A panel of officers presents a discussion of the special problems and stresses faced by Army families. Topics covered include transfers, separations, and what the Army is doing to meet family needs.

A Courageous Call to Freedom BR306—This speech by former President Ronald Reagan commemorates the fifty-fifth anniversary of D day. Parts of two patriotic speeches on June 6, 1984, at the fortieth anniversary of D day at Le Pointe du Hoc and Omaha Beach.

Is Your Parachute Packed? CT186—Captain Charlie Plumb talks about adversities in life, empowerment, and the choices people have to succeed, fail, or become victims. He relates the challenges he faced as a prisoner of war in Viet Nam to the challenges each of us faces in our daily lives.

"Lord, Keep Us Free" CT082—Maria Anne (Hansi) Hirschmann—This was a message given to military wives at Fort Stewart, Georgia, just before Operation Desert Storm. She describes growing up in a foster home in Czechoslovakia under the Nazi Third Reich, her years in Prague as a Hitler Youth leader, her time in and escape from a communist labor camp, and the help she received from the American troops in Germany.

"Love Healed My Wounds" CS377—Dave Roever shares his life story of marrying young and being sent to Viet Nam after joining the Navy. When a grenade exploded in his hand, he was disfigured. Assuming that no one could love him, he tried to commit suicide. His wife, Brenda, upon his return to the States, kissed his burned face and told him he was

loved. Dave encourages young people to resist negative peer pressure and to "hold on" through the tough times, because the good times will return.

The Marines: Raising the Standard of Excellence CT117—Gen. Charles Krulak (Ret), former commandant of the U.S. Marine Corps, talks about the Marines in light of "Generation X-ers," who: (1) desire boundaries; (2) are willing to be held accountable to well-defined boundaries; (3) will be followers; (4) can be leaders; and (5) want to be part of something easily identifiable that has some greatness to it.

Military Families CT133—Dr. James Dobson, a psychologist, talks with a panel about Focus on the Family's involvement with the military in addressing the needs of families.

A Patchwork Quilt of American Independence BR242—In celebration of Independence Day, this program features music, comments by service members from around the world, and historical quotes. There is also a dramatization that honors America's military.

The Price of Freedom CC015—This Adventures in Odyssey children's radio drama illustrates the truth that God is always in control, even in times of war, when it is difficult to know which side is right.

Remaining Faithful Against the Odds CT138—Deanna and Clebe McClary talk about their experiences, marriage, what America means to them, and how their faith was strengthened despite the fact that Clebe lost an eye and an arm in Vietnam.

Referrals

Military Ministry
6060 Jefferson Ave, Suite 6012
Newport News, VA 23605
(800) 444-6006 Ext. 286
www.milmin.com or E-mail: *donn.carlson@milmin.com*

This ministry is an outreach to all military families. Call and ask for their free, excellent resource called "Would You Like to Know God Personally?"

Navigators
PO Box 6000
Colorado Springs, CO 80934
(719) 594-2541
Fax: (719) 594-2447
E-mail: *milsupport@navigators.org*

www.navigators.org

This ministry is composed of over two hundred fifty staff and more than twelve hundred active-duty workers serving Army, Navy, Air Force, Marine Corps, and Coast Guard personnel on more than one hundred seventeen U.S. and overseas military bases and posts.

Officer's Christian Fellowship of the USA
3784 South Inca
Englewood, CO 80110
(303) 761-1984
(800) 424-1984
Fax: (303) 761-6226
E-mail: *ocfdenver@ocfhq.org*
www.ocfusa.org

The objectives of this fellowship are to build the spiritual maturity of member military officers and to provide support, especially for transient officers. A quarterly magazine, *Command,* is offered.

Military Community Youth Ministries
PO Box 2486
Colorado Springs, CO 80901-2484
(719) 381-1831
(800) 832-9098
Fax: (719) 381-1754
E-mail: *information@mcym.org*
www.mcym.org

By combining the vision and skills of Youth for Christ, Young Life, and Catholic Network Ministry, this group focuses on ministering to teens of military parents. Activities include Bible studies, camps, and retreats.

Cadence International
PO Box 1268
Englewood, CO 80150
(303) 762-1400
Fax: (303) 788-0661
E-mail: *hdqtrs@cadence.org*
www.cadence.org

With forty-two centers worldwide, this nonprofit organization reaches out to U.S. military singles, families, and youth. They do this through hospitality houses, retreat and Bible study ministries, and youth groups. The future looks bright for Cadence and for new ministry outreaches. Plans include concentrated ministries to people of color, dependent children, women in uniform, deployed persons and their families, as well as militaries of other nations.

Christian Military Fellowship (CMF)
PO Box 1207
Englewood, CO 80150-1207
(303) 761-1959
(800) 798-7875
Fax: (303) 761-4577
Fax: (800) 682-4206
E-mail: *admin@cmfhq.org*
www.cmfhq.org

This association is committed to reaching out to military members. CMF involves all elements of that society, including all ranks, family members, and civilian employees.

Digging the Well

We were told that Bob had orders to Saudi Arabia, and he was 95 percent sure he was going for a yearlong remote by himself. After waiting twelve weeks on the confirmation of the assignment, we discovered it had been canceled. Just this week we were told, again, that Bob has an assignment to Korea, and MPC (the assignments people) are about 95 percent sure he will go. Everything that I've written in this chapter was written for your benefit—and for mine. By the time this book is released, my Beloved may be in Korea for a year by himself, or he could be here with us, or we could all be stationed a half a world away. That is the nature of the life of a military family. It is frustrating at times, but it is vital that we continue to support our spouses in their commitment to our country.

I would like to leave you with the quote of a woman I greatly admire, Lenn Furrow. She has seen both sides of the military family fence—as an Army spouse and as the director of a family support center. Her words express briefly and powerfully why *you* are so important to the welfare of our nation and why *you* are the hero—the hero at home.

She says, "As soon as a family stops supporting the service member and is no longer willing to sacrifice, we will lose the best we have."

Digging the Well Before You Need It— the Family Checklist (recommended by the ACS/Family Program Coordinator)

Medical

- Get up-to-date immunizations for each family member.
- Know the location of health and dental records for each member.
- Know who is to be contacted in the case of a medical emergency.
- Know who has the medical power of attorney.

Finance

- Make sure there will be money immediately available on a continuing basis while the sponsor is gone.
- Set up an allotment to be sent to the family's bank and sign up for Sure-Pay/Direct Deposit.
- Will the direct deposit provide for all the necessities to maintain a household?
- If moving away from the installation during the deployment, is there money for this move?
- What types of accounts does the family have, and with what banks?
- Know where the bank books and account numbers are.
- Know if there is a safety deposit box and where the key is.
- Have credit card names and numbers written in a safe place along with the companies' numbers and addresses in the event of loss.
- Make sure the spouse knows how to manage and balance a checkbook.
- Establish a budget with information on the following payments and their schedules:
  1. Mortgage
  2. Telephone
  3. Water and sewage
  4. Electricity
  5. Trash
  6. Insurance
  7. Taxes
  8. Gas
  9. Credit cards

10. Auto payments
11. Other debts
- Know who is to be contacted regarding direct pay problems.

Automobile

- Know the responsibilities associated with the car.
- Know the name/address of lienholder.
- Locate the vehicle's title and make sure a copy of registration is in vehicle.
- Make sure the spouse is insured to drive the vehicle.
- Know renewal dates for license plates and safety inspection.
- Have a valid driver's license and know when it expires.
- Set aside a duplicate set of keys in a safe place.
- Become acquainted with how to make emergency repairs on a car (flat tire, overheating, dead battery, etc.).
- If spouse cannot drive, make arrangements for transportation.
- Know phone number of emergency transportation contact.

Housing

- Know where the following are located and how to use them:
  1. Electrical control box (fuse box), including how to replace fuses
  2. The water control valve for shutting off the water in case of an emergency (broken or leaking pipes)
  3. The gas control valve
  4. How to turn the water off on an overflowing toilet
  5. The name and phone number of repairmen
  6. Duplicate set of house keys

Legal/Administrative

- Have up-to-date identification cards.
- Know where and how the cards are replaced if lost or stolen.
- Have power of attorney of deploying member and how to use it to take necessary action regarding an important family matter or a special legal situation.
- Know where the power of attorney is kept.
- Have a copy of everyone's birth certificate.
- Have a copy of marriage license.
- Have copies of adoption papers, divorce decrees, court orders, and know where they are kept.

- Make sure everyone over the age of two has a social security number and know where they are kept.
- Know where the copies of state and federal income tax records are kept.
- Have copies of insurance policies.
- Know where any stocks, bonds, or securities are kept.
- Know where deeds to land are kept.
- Safeguard important papers (fire-safe box or safety deposit box at bank).
- Make sure wills are up-to-date for both spouses and know where they are kept.
- Send copies of wills to the person who will have guardianship of the children and to the person who will execute the will for your children and your spouse.
- Make sure base housing knows where the family member and deployed member can be located in the event of an emergency.
- Know where passports are kept.
- Have a current photo of all family members (full face, clearly visible) with information about height and weight.

★ ★ ★

On 9/11, while the president talked of war, all military bases went to "Delta Alert," the most severe alert possible. All leaves were canceled as we, along with the rest of the nation, held our breath and awaited orders from the Commander In Chief. As a fighter pilot and wife, Bob and I had long had our "affairs" in order. Yet this time I didn't expect my husband's reaction. Later that week Bob came home from flying, closed the doors to my home office, and sat on the couch. We were alone, and I waited for him to speak.

He looked as if he were carrying a heavy weight, his shoulders sagging under the pressure of the burden. He abruptly asked the question that was obviously bothering him. One that he had never asked before in our military lives together: "Beloved, what if I don't come back?"

I was surprised, because he'd always taken his job in stride. But there is something different about this war on terrorism. Suddenly I felt courage well up within me, the courage of many women who stood in my shoes decades before me as they sent their men into harm's way. The courage was one that had been molded in deep faith and perfected in the fire of fifteen years' experience.

I confidently answered him, "I believe you WILL come back, Beloved. I believe that if you go, you'll have a job to do over there—you'll fly and fight and accomplish your mission. But I believe God still has a job for you back here too. I believe you'll come back."

My conviction and faith acted as a balm for Bob. He let out a heavy sigh, relaxed his shoulders, and said, "All right." He had confidence in his wife's faith, and that's all he needed. He got up and left the room. His concerns quelled, he could now move on to the next task of the day: the perpetual search for his other black sock.

As soon as Bob left the room, I sensed another profound thought coming from deep within. It was a still, small voice, filled with comfort and grace. The words strangely held both reality and reassurance. But I knew they were thoughts I could *not* speak to Bob. Not then. Not there.

The simple words were: "And even if he doesn't come back, it will *still* be all right."

★   ★   ★

Learn as if you're going to live forever. Live as if you're going to die tomorrow.
> —JOHN WOODEN
> (Eddie Pells, AP Sports writer, "Wooden still living life's lessons," May 14, 2002)

Name: MSgt Perry Koehne

Spouse: MSgt Amy Koehne

Branch of Service: USAF

Kids: Kristina and Tairi Jo

Number of Moves: 6

Years in Service: 22 (18 since married)

Work: fire fighter, then occupational safety

Hobbies: motorcycles, scuba diving, graphic design, family

Least Favorite Aspect of Military Life: being separated from Amy and kids. Not being in control of the next step of our lives. Having to plan with options 2, 3, and 4 in mind, because everyone else has other plans for you. Long hours.

Favorite Aspect of Military Life: constant challenges

CHAPTER EIGHTEEN

Hidden Hero Portrait— Perry Koehne

Dynamic "Dual Spouse" Duo

~

*P**erry, "PK" to his friends, is an active-duty service member married to another active-duty member, which is referred to as a "dual spouse" marriage. There are many such couples in the U.S. Armed Forces, and their situations are rife with challenge. How does this couple rise to meet those challenges? I was curious to know and interviewed Perry to get his perspective.*

How do you cope with Amy's demanding career in conjunction with your own?

PK: It is day-to-day give-and-take! We do it with a lot of patience, love, prayer, and forgiveness. It never goes perfectly. Never. But we try to expect the unexpected! We take turns supporting one another. We gently remind each other when we see the other getting off track or out of balance in our career. We aren't perfect, and there are times when we reach the burnout zone, but now that we have Christ in our lives, we reach quickly to the One who can pull us in and carry the burden that we can't.

Can you give us some specifics on what you mean by "give-and-take?"

PK: Here is the SECRET: We feel you can't have your cake and eat it too! Here's an example:

(1) If you both try to have the perfect career, both of you will lose.

We have seen so many examples of military couples attempting perfection and for a time *seem* to achieve success. But then as quickly as they achieve greatness in the eyes of their peers, they can't maintain the pace and succumb to the stress, temptation, or physical strain. So many of our friends have divorced for various reasons, but all were directly related to how they managed their dual military careers and home life.

(2) You must pick and choose your victories.

Not everything the military asks you to do will mesh with your family goals or values. You have to know where your family stands without the military, and then build the military into your family's life—not the other way around. When Amy and I became NCOs, we were expected to attend our squadron and group functions. When Christmas rolls around, and you're expected to juggle four unit parties, two work parties, two school parties, a couple of orchestra recitals, and a church play in two weeks, there is no way everyone can win!

Amy and I discuss who wins and who loses. It is always based on family first, and *then* we discuss which of us needs the support *most* right now. And guess what? We don't go to all of them! Home is still where the heart is!

It's not only events either; it's a daily battle. From stuffy noses, birthdays, dental appointments, and softball games to family vacations, the AF tries really hard to tell you how much they care. But it's still all about the mission, and it's ultimately up to us to make the hard choices for our family.

How has Amy's recent honor of becoming a first sergeant impacted your lives?

PK: Since Amy took on the role of first sergeant, it has placed a new level of stress on our family. It's a commitment we understood before she decided to take the plunge, and we gladly supported her because she selflessly supported all of us for several years when my job overshadowed our lives.

Background: In 1994, I was told that the AF had too many fire fighters, and I was forced to retrain after ten years from a career that I loved into something completely new. Amy was also happy in her work of instructing AF students on how to maintain computer mainframe systems. My new job would mean a new move, and she would have to leave a job she loved.

I retrained into occupational safety, and we were given orders to Holloman AFB (Oh, no! The desert! We had never even *visited* the desert! *And* I'm a water person!)

Without reservation, Amy supported me with all of her heart. When she wanted to become a first sergeant, we sat down as a family, weighed the cost, and decided to support *her* completely.

How do you maintain stability for your daughters?

PK: If you had asked me this question seven years ago, I would have said, "HUH?" And then I would tell you that we were doing the best we could and hoping for the best! It wasn't until Amy and I gave our lives to the Lord that we found forgiveness for our sins and could truly raise our kids with a solid foundation. The stability we are able to offer our children now comes from the Maker of the Universe. Now, regardless of whether we stay in one place or travel around the world, as long as we teach them right from wrong and share our trust in God, they are going to be fine—no matter what the world throws their way.

Obviously, the role of faith enters into the equation for you and Amy. Has faith always been a strong part of your military lifestyle?

PK: Our faith was built while in the military, so it's a part of us and our career. Our faith has gotten us through everything we've done and continues to keep us going day by day. God chose us! When we got orders to New Mexico, Amy and I brought the girls to Alamogordo to look for a house and found the one we wanted right next to a church. That church ended up becoming our church home, our girls found a Christian school, and we had the support of a network of people while we pursued our dual spouse military careers.

What are you most proud of in Amy—specifically regarding her career?

PK: Amy has the most incredible ability to energize teams toward goals and objectives and motivate them to be their best, in spite of set-backs and obstacles. She always gives her very best to everything she does. But I'm most proud of the stand she takes for Christ while at work.

What is the longest period of time she's been away from home?

PK: She deployed to Prince Sultan, Saudi Arabia, from June through October of 1999, during Desert Shield. It was a tough time, but the girls pulled me through it! Structure, special home improvement projects, weekend hiking trips, a lot of communication with Amy; and God sustained us.

What is the longest time you've been away?

PK: I spent one year at Osan Air Base, Republic of Korea, 1996/1997. That was a long and difficult year, but our transition back home was much smoother than I expected. This was largely due to the roles Amy and I took straight from the Bible, where she relinquished family leadership to me, and I cherished her and openly praised her and the girls for keeping the family together during hard times.

What is the most gratifying part of your career?

Amy: I've had four different jobs while I've been in the Air Force. I would have never been able to experience and enjoy such a wide variety of careers in a "normal" life. My best jobs were as an instructor and now as a first sergeant.

PK: The friendships! Also the unbelievable opportunity to meet so many wonderful people and to be a small part of their lives. As I look back after twenty years, so many people kept telling me, "Slow down; you're overdoing it; you didn't have to do that." Now I still have the same answer: I place service before self. This is part of the Air Force core values, and Jesus said it too, so it must be important. It is not easy to serve, but it's the greatest part of life.

What are some of the family things you do together?

PK: Camping, hiking, church, choir, youth groups, plays, road trips. Spur-of-the-moment activities are the best—we just like to get lost and see what adventure lies ahead! We also like shopping, movie nights at home, board games, special projects, and serving each other gourmet meals at home.

Have you ever feared for your children's welfare as dual spouse military members?

PK: Once. We were both stationed in Panama during the Manuel Noriega uprising. We were taking our two-year-old daughter, Kristina, to a doctor's appointment at the Gorgas Army hospital. To get there, we had to leave Howard AFB and cross the Bridge of the Americas. Unbeknownst to us, there was a heated demonstration going on, which had the potential of turning into an all-out riot (as often happened during those times). We were stuck on the bridge in our Honda, and the baby was in her car seat in the back. We turned to our right and saw a row of "Panamanian Militia." These were untrained citizens ranging in age from sixteen to seventy, who had been given M-16s! As they stood only inches away from our baby, all we could think was, *Why are we doing this? Why are we in the military with a child?* Because we were dual spouse with a child, we were sent to another duty station stateside—only two weeks before the Panamanian invasion!

If you had to do the "dual spouse" thing all over again—would you?

Amy: Only with PK. I can't imagine doing it with anybody else.

PK: Ummmm . . . you asked the wrong person. I would always take the alternate route just to see what it was like. I would gladly follow Amy around if she wanted to be in the military all over again. I think I would try my hand in the corporate world or design 3-D animation or make movies. I would definitely seek God earlier in my life than I did.

It's quite evident from PK and Amy's interview that faith plays a major role in their ability to juggle the joys and job of a dual military spouse existence. They are not alone. God and country have long been a major part of every American military branch since our nation was founded, and each branch of the service has chaplains and chapel programs for every faith.

PK and Amy are not only involved in their church, they are highly involved in their community and in a wide variety of volunteer efforts as well. Their example of hidden heroes is inspirational to the people who cross their paths both professionally and personally. They are definitely a dynamic dual spouse duo!

CHAPTER NINETEEN

Ruffles and Flourishes

A Salute to the Hero at Home

⌒

*J*enny's husband was not yet deployed, but he was putting in long hours due to the recent terrorist attacks on the World Trade Center and the Pentagon. Jenny had a problem, and she knew she had to handle it alone: her driver's side window was broken and would not roll down. This may not sound like a big problem to you, but Jenny lived on base and had to roll that window down as she passed the guard sentry about twenty-five times a day! Her husband was flying his F-117 Stealth Fighter that day and could not come to her rescue.

In the midst of her frustration, Jenny reminded herself that she was a former military member who used to be an air weapons controller, and she of all people should know how to handle a pesky problem. Her mind drifted back to when she was stationed in Korea and had just come off shift but still had her radio headset on. Word came that a jet had gone down. Jenny counted up the number of pilots that had checked in and realized that it was a jet that was on final approach.

Jenny watched the radar screen and saw the "blips" of search helicopters searching for the wreckage at the departure end of the runway! She was only a lieutenant, but she knew one end of the flight line from the other! She radioed the search-and-rescue team and said, "If the F-16 was on arrival, perhaps you should leave the departure end of the runway and search the arrival end!" Almost comically, she watched the blips on her radar move from the departure end of the runway to the arrival end. By the time the helicopters found the jet, it was burning in a rice patty. Miraculously, the pilot had escaped safely and was being chased down the road by an angry rice farmer!

Yes, problem solving was Jenny's specialty! So back to reality and back to the car window. She quickly devised a "Plan A," which was to send her five-year-old to school with the carpool, pack up her two-year-old in the van, and drive to the dealership. She had it all planned out: She called the dealership, confirmed that a courtesy van could take her home, and made sure they could fix her car in one day. They would leave the keys under the seat, and she'd pick up the vehicle after hours.

Jenny implemented Operation Window at 0800 hours. She checked into the service department and asked if there would be a driver to take her home.

"Yes, Mrs. Ott. Sure thing, Mrs. Ott. No problem, Mrs. Ott!"

She took her daughter, Kelly, outside to sit on a bench and enjoy the sunny New Mexico morning.

The five minutes turned into two hours. By that time, Kelly had eaten all her Cheerios, finished drinking the "Pessi" that Jenny had succumbed to buying her, and was lobbing her dolly across the parking lot, trying to hit a new car. When Jenny took the dolly away, Kelly threw herself down on the ground and started screaming, throwing an all-out tantrum.

It was time for "Plan B." She would buy Kelly a KING-SIZED chocolate bar from the vending machine, take her to the showroom floor, and make a desperate threat: "Either you get me a courtesy van, or I'll turn my kid loose on the velour interior of the new Sebring convertible!" She had just walked into the showroom floor, Kelly and candy in tow, and was about to make her announcement, when another announcement came to her rescue:

"Anyone waiting for a courtesy van, please come to the showroom."

Jenny grabbed Kelly and all her gear and arrived, breathless, at the service center to find another unhappy surprise—the "courtesy van." Jenny describes the moment of truth: "I almost dropped my kid in disbelief! This had to have been the first minivan ever off the production line. I mean, all the other dealerships in town had shiny new courtesy vans with fancy signs on them, and I had to get stuck with this rust bucket. This was not a courtesy van, this was a dis-courtesy van!"

The only thing older than the minivan was . . . the driver! She checked with him to make sure he could get on base with all the heightened security requirements, and he replied, "Yep," and then spat out the window.

After strapping in Kelly's car seat with the only working seat belt in the backseat, she firmly instructed her, "Don't touch anything!"

When Jenny went to close the passenger side of the van, she discovered that it was dented and wouldn't shut all the way. She said, "It smelled like the inside of a country-western bar, and I could see the road out the one-inch gap at the bottom of the door." She felt safer when she was strapped in a T-37 jet on an incentive ride than she did in that van. After the third attempt, the "ancient of days" finally got it started.

No problem. Jenny was a trooper. By the time they got to the base, the line was backed up for twenty minutes to go through the barricades and security points. They got to the sentry, and she showed him her identification card.

The young airman asked the older man if he had an identification card, and the old man replied, "Nope!" and spat in the opposite direction.

The "kid" at the gate looked at Jenny and said, "I can't let this van on base; you're going to have to get out."

"What?" Jenny cried in disbelief.

"Get out!" he repeated with indifference.

"That's real nice," she replied. "My husband is still flying; I'll have to hoof it home!"

It was now time for "Plan C." Jenny gathered up Kelly, the car seat, the diaper bag, Kelly's dolly, the dolly's bottle, the dolly's blanket, and hauled everything toward the gate in order to hike the two miles to her house in the middle of ninety-plus degree New Mexico heat with a screaming toddler in tow.

No problem.

As she approached the gate, the second sentry asked her what she was doing, and she told him.

"With a baby?" he asked incredulously. "He threw you out with a baby?"

He made a quick call to headquarters and then said, "Wait here in the guard shack; we'll get a car to drive you home."

Jenny describes "Plan D" in her typically upbeat way: "I felt like a Wal-Mart greeter standing in the guard shack as Kelly waved to all the cars that passed by. After another half hour of waiting, a police car drove up. It felt really weird strapping the car seat into the back of the police car."

As soon as she walked in the door of her house, the phone rang. She answered it to hear her husband's voice:

"Hey, baby, I just landed! How did it go?"

★   ★   ★

When Jenny was on active duty, she got a number of medals, including the Air Force Achievement medal, the National Defense medal, and the Combat Readiness medal. But I believe she deserves a medal for the basics of holding down the fort (or the guard shack!) while her husband was flying, training to defend our nation.

Jenny has also been handed another major challenge in the past year: melanoma cancer. While understandably concerned, Jenny is not panic-stricken. She is finding the strength in her family and faith to be able to rise to this challenge. Her attitude remains positive as she says, "The good news is it's *in-fitu,* which means that the cancer is contained within the mole and hasn't spread to any other organs."

Jenny isn't alone. You experience your own kind of challenges every week. You rise to the task even though you don't wear the rank. You haven't taken the oath. And you often stand alone (or with a few babies on your hips). I *wish* I could give every last one of you a medal!

In the military, there is a tradition that offers "Ruffles and Flourishes" to Very Important People. This is a musical honor reserved for general officers and equivalent ranking officials. At the 10th Mountain Division, they had a ceremony that was similar in that it paid special honor to high-ranking division officers. They called it a "tattoo." Bob and I witnessed the majesty of this event several times, and it was singularly impressive. Every military member is in his/her formal dress uniforms, there's a red carpet for guests of honor, and their spouses are in formal attire, standing with them on the carpet. A full band plays music that makes our hearts beat with pride and brings tears to our eyes.

A Salute

If you will indulge me for a minute, I'd like to salute you, the military spouse, with your own special event. But I'll need your cooperation.

I would like you to imagine with me a special dream scene: *You* are the one standing on that carpet. This tribute is to the homeland hero.

Your spouse is dressed formally in respect for *you* tonight, his eyes filled with pride as he looks at you lovingly. If his buttons were not sewn on tightly, they would surely burst.

Your spouse starts the series of toasts: "I propose a toast!" He smiles at you proudly and holds out his champagne glass. "To her bravery and courage in the face of uncertainty and doubt."

"Hear, Hear!" the audience replies. "To bravery and courage!"

The congressman in the audience is next: "I propose a toast!" He looks into your eyes and speaks with polish and confidence. "To her strength and valor above and beyond the call of duty!"

The crowd shouts a hearty "Hear, Hear!" as the sound of crystal tapping crystal is heard. "To strength and valor!"

Suddenly you hear the band strike up "Hail to the Chief" as the audience ripples with gasps of astonishment!

The Commander In Chief himself suddenly parts the crowd as he strides purposefully toward you, his Secret Servicemen following at a safe distance. He motions for silence:

"I'd like to propose a toast!" The audience is spellbound, awaiting the words of the most powerful man in the world.

"I'm from the Lone Star State," he drawls in a slight Texas accent, immediately putting everyone at ease. "And I'm here to pay honor to the 'lone star' in this room." He looks into your astonished face and smiles a warm grin that makes you feel as if you're the only one in the room.

He holds his champagne glass high and shouts boldly to the crowd, "I propose a toast!" Everyone raises their glass. "To the Hero at Home! *America* salutes you!"

At Thermopylae, a rocky mountain pass in northern Greece, the feared and admired Spartan soldiers stood three hundred strong. Theirs was a suicide mission, to hold the pass against the invading millions of the mighty Persian Army. Day after bloody day they withstood the terrible onslaught, buying time for the Greeks to rally their forces. Born into a cult of spiritual courage, physical endurance, and unmatched battle skill, the Spartans would be remembered for the greatest military stand in history. . . .

[The King speaks to Dienekes, a woman who has lost both husband and son in the siege.]

"The city speculates, my lady," King Leonidas resumes, "as to why I elected those I did to the three hundred. . . . But I now tell you.

"I chose them not for their own valor, but for that of their women. . . . When the battle is over, when the three hundred have gone down to death, then will all Greece look to the Spartans, to see how they bear it.

"But who, lady, who will the Spartans look to? To you. To you, the other wives, daughters, sisters, and mothers of the fallen.

"If they behold your hearts riven and broken with grief, they, too, will break. And Greece will break with them. But if you bear up, dry-eyed, not alone enduring your loss but seizing it with contempt for its agony and embracing it as the honor that it is in truth, then Sparta will stand. And all Hellas will stand behind her. . . . You and your sisters of the Three Hundred are the mothers now of all Greece and of freedom itself."

—From *Gates of Fire* by Steven Pressfield
(Bantam Books, 1999)

Anstett, Patricia. "Do You Need More Sleep?" from *The Oregonian,* 1999.

Army Family Team Building Levels I, II, III. Department of the Army, 2000.

Farrell, Pam. *Men Are Like Waffles—Women Are Like Spaghetti.* Harvest House, 2001.

Fishback, Jim. *Defending the Military Marriage.* Family Life Publications, 2002.

Gray, Alice, et al. *Lists to Live By.* Multnomah, 1999.

Kay, Ellie. *Shop, Save, and Share.* Bethany House Publishers, 1998.

———. *How to Save Money Every Day.* Bethany House Publishers, 2001.

———. *Money Doesn't Grow On Trees.* Bethany House Publishers, 2002.

MetLife. *All-Season Exercise.* MetLife Consumer Education Center, 2000.

Miller, Susan. *After the Boxes Are Unpacked.* Focus on the Family Publishing, 1995.

O'Leary, Col. Jeffrey. *Taking the High Ground.* Cook, 2001.

Pressfield, Steven. *Gates of Fire.* Bantam Books, 1999.

Stack, Debi. *Martha to the Max.* Moody Press, 2000.

Swindoll, Chuck. *Tale of the Tardy Oxcart.* Word Publishing, 1998.

———. *Strengthening Your Grip.* Word Publishing, 1983.